English Works 3

**John Catron,
Chris Marshall
and Jo Shackleton**

Hodder & Stoughton

A MEMBER OF THE HODDER HEADLINE GROUP

Copyright text:
pp. 3–4 © BBC; pp. 5, 7, 8, 12 © Banbury Guardian/Banbury Citizen; p. 7 © TES; pp. 20, 23 extracts from *Flowers for Algernon* by Daniel Keynes, published by Victor Gollancz; p. 22 extract from *The Yellow Wall Paper* by Charlotte Perkins Gilman; pp. 23, 25, 28, 33, 34 extract from *The Tell-Tale Heart* by Edgar Allan Poe, published by Random House, New York; pp. 29, 30 extracts from *Stone Cold* © Robert Swindells, Penguin; p. 35, 'A Martian Sends A Postcard Home' by Craig Raine, published in *Collected Poems 1978–1998* published by Picador; pp. 44, 45, 46 extracts from Ellen MacArthur's log, printed in *Guardian Unlimited* © Kingfisher; p. 47, 49 extracts from article by Euan Ferguson, printed in the *Observer* © Guardian Newspapers Limited; p. 54 © 1999–2001 The American Museum of Natural History; p. 55 The Antarctic Connection LLC; p. 57 text and photo © Tasmanian Museum and Art Gallery; p. 58 © 2001 Tribe City Group Inc.; p. 60 *Twenty Thousand Leagues Under the Sea* is published by Penguin Books; pp. 131–2 extract from *Out of Bounds* by Beverley Naidoo; p. 138 'Somehow we survive' by Dennis Brutus from *A Simple Lust/Sirens, Knuckles, Boots* – Heinemann African Writers Series/Mbari Press, Ibadan, Nigeria; p. 139 © Linton Kwesi Johnson, reproduced by kind permission of LKJ Music Publishers Ltd.; p. 140 Copyright 1973 Fifty-Six Hope Road Music Limited/Odnil Music Limited/Blue Mountain Music Limited/Stuck on Music/Embassy Music/Cherry Lane Music Publishing Company Incorporated, USA (3.13%). All rights controlled and administered by Rykomusic Limited, (93.75%) Campbell Connelly & Company Limited, (3.12%). Used by Permission of Music Sales Limited. All Rights Reserved. International Copyright Secured; p. 142 'Letter From Mama Dot' from MAMA DOT by Fred D'Aguiar published by Chatto & Windus. Used by permission of The Random House Group Limited; p. 145 extract from *A Long Walk to Freedom* by Nelson Mandela, published by Time Warner Books UK.

Copyright photographs:
pp. 2 and 3 © Tim Ockenden/PA Photos 2002; p. 19 photos of *Harry Potter and the Philosopher's Stone* and *The Silence of the Lambs* © The Ronald Grant Archive, photo of *The Lord of the Rings* © New Line Cinema/The Ronald Grant Archive; p. 32 © Thom Lang/Corbis; p. 33 © Joseph Sohm; ChronoSohm Inc./Corbis; p. 41 © Frank Hurley/Royal Geographical Society; p. 45 © European Press Agency/PA Photos 2003; p. 47 © Stefan Rousseau/PA Photos 2003; p. 51 © Frank Hurley/Royal Geographical Society; p. 52 © Underwood & Underwood/Corbis; p. 55 © Nick Briggs; pp. 78, 80 supplied by John Catron; p. 82 (top) © Yann Arthus-Bertrand/Corbis, (bottom) © Donald Cooper/Photostage; p. 96 © Donald Cooper/Photostage; p. 99 © Donald Cooper/Photostage; p. 105 © Adam Woolfitt/Corbis; pp. 115, 116 © Herbie Knott; p. 126 photo supplied by HarperCollins; p. 127 © Gillian Cargill, (bottom) © Peter Williams/Corbis; p. 128 (top) © Jon Super/Redferns, (bottom) © Corbis; p. 137 © photo of Dennis Brutus supplied by Sunni Elliott; p. 139 photo of Grace Nichols supplied by Curtis Brown Ltd, photo of Amryl Johnson supplied by Virago, photo of Linton Kwesi Johnson supplied by PA Photos; p. 140 © Jeff Albertson/CORBIS; p. 142 © Claire McNamee; p. 144 © Flip Schulke/Corbis; p. 145 © Peter Turnley/Corbis.

Copyright artwork:
pp. 11, 15, 17, 19, 23, 25, 39, 40, 70, 82, 106, 114 and 119 © Ben Hasler.
pp. 18, 21, 25, 26, 35, 37, 38, 98 and 132 © Ruth Thomlevold.

Contributors:
Unit 1: Chris Marshall
Unit 2: Maria Cox and Samantha Marshall
Unit 3: Alan Howe
Unit 4: Lucy Lawrence
Unit 5: Karyn Taylor and Vickie Phillips
Unit 6: Ruth Turner
Unit 7: Karyn Taylor and Vickie Phillips
Unit 8: Jo Shackleton

Every effort has been made to trace copyright holders of material reproduced in this book. Any rights not acknowledged here will be acknowledged in subsequent printings if notice is given to the publisher.

Orders: please contact Bookpoint Ltd, 130 Milton Park, Abingdon, Oxon OX14 4SB. Telephone: (+44) 01235 827720. Fax: (44) 01235 400454. Lines are open from 9.00–6.00, Monday to Saturday, with a 24 hour message answering service. You can also order through our website www.hodderheadline.co.uk.

British Library Cataloguing in Publication Data
A catalogue record for this title is available from the British Library

ISBN 0 340 87251 9

First Published 2003
Impression number   10 9 8 7 6 5 4 3 2 1
Year   2007 2006 2005 2004 2003

Copyright © 2003 John Catron, Chris Marshall and Jo Shackleton

All rights reserved. No part of this publication may be reproduced or transmitted in any form or by any means, electronic or mechanical, including photocopy, recording, or any information storage and retrieval system, without permission in writing from the publisher or under licence from the Copyright Licensing Agency Limited. Further details of such licences (for reprographic reproduction) may be obtained from the Copyright Licensing Agency Limited, of 90 Tottenham Court Road, London W1T 4LP.

Cover photo from Eyewire/Getty Images
Typeset by Pantek Arts Ltd, Maidstone, Kent, ME14 1NY
Printed in Italy for Hodder & Stoughton Educational, a division of Hodder Headline, 338 Euston Road, London NW1 3BH.

Contents

Unit 1	Who's responsible?	1
Unit 2	On the edge	17
Unit 3	Testing times	41
Unit 4	Taking control	65
Unit 5	Exploring scenes from Shakespeare	81
Unit 6	Taking a trip?	105
Unit 7	Under your skin	125
Unit 8	Self review	149

UNIT 1 Who's responsible?

KEY OBJECTIVES

In this unit you will learn about the following key objectives:

Standard English – using formal spoken English to explain your ideas and opinions

Identify underlying issues – deciding what issues are raised by a radio programme

Considered viewpoint – discussing evidence before deciding on your own view

Counter-argument – identifying weaknesses in someone else's argument and providing an alternative written viewpoint of your own

---

In May 2002 a mother, Ms Patricia Amos, was sentenced to 60 days in prison because of her teenage daughters' truancy from school. This decision by Banbury Magistrates' Court was believed to be the first of its kind since new powers were introduced in November 2000. The daughters' truancy was particularly severe. Emma attended only 55 out of a total of 190 school registrations (29%). Her younger sister's attendance was slightly better: 64 out of 190 registrations (34%).

Ms Amos decided to appeal against her sentence. Her appeal was successful and Oxford Crown Court agreed that she should be released after serving 28 days.

Opinion was divided about the rights and wrongs of the court's initial decision. Some felt strongly that it was right for a mother to be punished for her daughters' truancy. Others felt that effective action should have been taken earlier to avoid the court case ever arising. A lot of parents felt that young people themselves should take responsibility for getting themselves to school.

This unit will involve you looking closely at this case and deciding on your own views about who should be held responsible for pupils' attendance at school.

English Works

Ms Amos outside Oxford Crown Court.

Shortly after the release of Ms Amos, Radio 4's *Today* programme carried out an in-depth interview with her. The main part of the interview focused on how her daughters' truancy became so severe.

A good radio or television interviewer will not only probe the views of the interviewee but also make the listener or viewer think carefully about the issues under discussion and their own viewpoint. Next you will listen to a recording of the interview with Ms Amos and be asked to think about the issues her case raises. A transcript of the interview is provided on the following page.

TASK

1 Listen carefully to the recording of the radio interview. You may want to follow it using the transcript.

2 Listen to it a second time. This time note some of the different issues that you think are raised by the case. Your notes may look like the following example:

> *Patricia Amos interview – issues*
> - *Perhaps important letters from schools about truancy should be followed up with a phone call to the parents/guardians to check they have been received*
> - *Schools should devise an advice booklet for parents suggesting what they should do if they are concerned about truancy*

3 In a pair, talk about the different issues you have noted. You may wish to add new issues to your notes. Decide on your two most important issues.

4 Report your most important issues to the rest of the class. Again, note any further interesting points made by other members of the class.

English Works

Who's Responsible?

Radio 4 interview with Ms. Amos

Interviewer: Tell us how things got so bad because the two of them start skiving off school... the school get in contact with you to go to meetings many times and you don't go to any of them. Why did you ignore the problem?

Patricia Amos: I haven't had half of the letters or the visits that they say I have. I mean they left a summons for me to go to court with a 12 year old... that had been truanting school. Now how responsible is that? They left a court summons with my Jackie for me to attend court... which I never received. And yet she hadn't been going to school.

Interviewer: But you saying you never, because when you look down the list from November year of 2000, in fact before then, the summons to various meetings with education officials, with social workers, with, parenting meetings at school, it goes on for months and months...

Patricia Amos: Yep. Half of them I didn't even know anything about. Well a majority of them.

Interviewer: You knew there was a problem though?

Patricia Amos: I had my suspicions yeah but I think... in, up here wasn't functioning properly and I think I should have sought help a lot sooner.

Interviewer: What, you were just, you were turning a blind eye?

Patricia Amos: Yeah, basically yeah.

Interviewer: Can you see that the school had little alternative?

Patricia Amos: Erm... well nobody had any alternative did they. I mean I caused my own problem really at the end of the day and now I've suffered for it, my children have suffered for it and hopefully, well I know for a fact that something good has come out of something bad.

Interviewer: So... the system works?

Ms Amos with her solicitor outside court.

English Works

Patricia Amos: Yeah. Yeah. It has worked, it's worked for me. I can assure you I will be everywhere I'm meant to be, I will liaise with my daughter and my solicitor every other day to make sure, 'til I get myself back on going home, sorting things out. I'm going to make sure that every day somebody knows I have taken them to school, or I have put them in a taxi to school and I'm gonna phone the school and make sure they're there, I'm gonna go out of my way 'cos there's no way I wanna spend anymore time in prison, no way.

Interviewer: But did you have to go to prison to find that out?

Patricia Amos: Erm, I think, yeah, I think I did because I think it would have just got worse. It woke up and made me realise that I am a parent and not just a sister or auntie, you know something like that, they're my children.

Interviewer: How did you feel when you heard that you were being sent to prison?

Patricia Amos: Well. Huh. Shocked. Very shocked … very shocked indeed.

Interviewer: What was it like?

Patricia Amos: Horrible.

[pause]

Interviewer: So what happens now?

Patricia Amos: Well, hopefully, when all this has died down, I'm gonna go home and get my act together. Make sure that I am on top of everything that is going on around me.

Interviewer: But do you know that you can be when you think of everything that has been going on in the past?

Patricia Amos: Oh, I know that I definitely can be yes. Oh yeah… I've got no choice. They are my children, they are my responsibility and they need their full-time education and I'm going to make sure that they get what little bit of time they've got left in time in full.

Interviewer: So do you feel angry when you look back at all of this?

Patricia Amos: Angry with myself yeah, for being so stupid and you know they've lost. Well their childhood has been whipped away from them for, for my fault.

Who's Responsible?

In the next part of the unit, you will be looking more closely at different viewpoints expressed about the Patricia Amos case. Having studied the different arguments and the evidence available, you will need to decide on your own considered viewpoint.

Below is the front page report covering the release of Ms Amos from prison. It comes from a local paper, the *Banbury Citizen*:

Warnings go out as mum freed

Amos case held up as lesson to all

EDUCATION chiefs would not think twice about prosecuting 'inadequate' mum Patricia Amos if her children missed school again.

The 43-year-old, of School View in Banbury, was sent to prison for allowing her daughters to play truant. She was released on Wednesday after her sentence was cut from 60 days to 28 at Oxford Crown Court. Having already served half that time she was freed. She is now staying with relatives.

Amos hit the headlines when she became the first person in Britain to be jailed for failing to educate her children properly.

Keith Mitchell, leader of Oxfordshire County Council which brought the prosecution, said: "This is a warning we mean business on truancy. It is the parents' responsibility to get their children to school and there are no excuses.

"We hope she will not re-offend, but if she does fail again she will be sent to prison again."

Cllr Mitchell said the council had received a letter of support from education minister Estelle Morris.

Sue Aldridge, acting principal education social worker with the council, said the prosecution had worked as Amos's daughters, Jackie, 13, and Emma, 15, had returned to school.

She said: "The girls have been in school except one day when they went to visit their mum and one day when the younger one was ill. That is excellent. It is all we ever wanted."

PC Rebecca Burnell, North Oxfordshire area police youth liaison officer, said truancy in the area had fallen because of the publicity surrounding the case.

Amos's daughters had missed lessons at Banbury School for the best part of two years. She was sentenced to prison on May 9.

Judge Peter Crawford told Amos her sentence had been longer than necessary.

Louise Warton, prosecuting, said numerous meetings had been called before prosecution, but Mrs Amos and her daughters had failed to attend.

Amos's counsel, Paul Reid, described the sentence as 'draconian' and said the last few years of her life had been marred by her mother's death and her partner's alcoholism.

Slashing the sentence Judge Crawford said: "You are the mother of two girls and they depend on you to make sure they are properly brought up and educated.

"It is not their responsibility to get themselves to school, it is yours.

"The court regarded this as a bad case. A sentence of imprisonment was the only one."

Amos's solicitor Stephen Warrington said she was pleased to be free.

He said: "She is delighted to be out and very grateful for the support and interest she received."

The newspaper report includes brief quotations giving the viewpoints of various people involved in the case. For example, the fourth paragraph features a quotation from the leader of the Oxfordshire County Council, Keith Mitchell, who is responsible for ensuring rates of truancy are kept to a minimum in his region:

❚❚ **This is a warning we mean business on truancy. It is the parents' responsibility to get their children to school and there are no excuses.**

We hope she will not re-offend, but if she does fail again she will be sent to prison again. ❚❚

His view is very clear: he approves of the prison sentence and thinks responsibility for attendance at schools lies with parents.

TASK

Read through a copy of the report and highlight the comments made by each of the main people involved. Then, using a grid like the one below, sum up each viewpoint in your own words:

Person involved	Viewpoint
Sue Aldridge	
PC Rebecca Burnell	
Paul Reid	
Judge Peter Crawford	
Stephen Warrington	

Later on in the unit you may wish to return to these viewpoints and refer to them in your work.

English Works

Who's Responsible?

Next you are going to look closely at three more detailed points of view about the case. Each writer develops a particular line of thought. Read each of the following texts:

Text 1

An editorial from the *Times Educational Supplement*, an educational newspaper aimed at teachers.

Wrong message

THE drug dealers and shoplifters in Holloway prison must have been astonished when Patricia Amos arrived last week, jailed for two months for failing to send her teenage daughters to school. The media reaction suggests the rest of us are equally surprised.

Estelle Morris may think the case sends the right message but it's difficult to believe that jailing the sole carer of two children is any better an idea than docking child benefit from parents of young offenders. And how often must mothers be locked up to perpetuate "the right message?"

Maybe the message is the problem. "Send your kids to school or we'll send you to prison" is hardly reasoned discourse. Who helps parents of truants, often themselves school failures, to see what education promises? The Sure Start scheme for disadvantaged families is a long-term approach: parents with truants today need positive help, not prison.

Text 2

A letter to a local newspaper, the *Banbury Guardian*.

FURTHER to your coverage of the case of Patricia Amos (*Banbury Guardian*, May 16), can I point out that it is not illegal to keep your children out of school, it is illegal not to provide them with an education.

Section 7 of the Education Act 1996 states: The parent of every child of compulsory school age shall cause him to receive efficient full-time education suitable; a. to his age, ability, and aptitude, and b. to any special educational needs he may have, either by regular attendance at school or otherwise.

Without embarrassing my eldest daughter by being too specific, we decided together that her educational needs would be best met by studying at home. Her education is efficient as she is the only child in the class, studying things she has chosen and is interested in. Her education is geared entirely to her age, ability and aptitude, as we have no one else to consider. It suits us just fine.

If any one would like more information Education Otherwise has a website at www.education-otherwise.org. Home Education Advisory Service has a website at www.heas.org.uk.

I can also recommend a book called *Free Range Education*; *How home education works*, edited by Terri Dowty, Hawthorn Press.

I feel it is important that people know what the law actually says. Obviously home education is hard work for parents and there are pros and cons just as there are with school, but families should be aware that they have the freedom to take responsibility for the education of their children in whichever way suits them best.

It makes me sad to see children who are not thriving in school for whatever reason, being forced to continue attending in the mistaken belief that they have to go by law. I don't wish to comment specifically on the Amos case but it is equally sad to see children wasting their abilities by receiving no education at all. I wish the Amos family good luck and hope the girls do well with their future education.

Text 3

An article from the *Banbury Guardian* that includes comments from a father, Mr Paul Hawkins.

Children should be punished not parents, insists dad

A FATHER, who was taken before Banbury magistrates when his daughter refused to go to school, says truanting children should be punished and not their parents.

Paul Hawkins appeared in court in April at the same time as Patricia Amos who went on to be jailed two weeks ago.

Now he has called for boarding schools to deal with difficult children.

He and his partner Deborah French were given a conditional discharge by Banbury magistrates when their 16-year-old daughter Jenna did not attend school.

Miss French, 34, and Mr Hawkins, 35, of Howard Road in Grimsbury, worked with social services to get Jenna back into education after she refused to go to Banbury School for a year because of bullying.

Eventually she was offered a place at Warriner School in Bloxham but after a few months she began playing truant again without her parents' knowledge.

It was then that the couple were taken to court.

Mr Hawkins told the *Banbury Guardian*: "They should think of something else other than sending people to jail. They should punish the kids."

TASK

1. Working in pairs, re-read each text.
2. Decide on the overall viewpoint of each writer and sum it up in a few words.

3. Then identify the main points or evidence used by each writer to justify his or her point of view.
4. Discuss these points and evidence and decide on whether you agree with them or not – and why! Use a copy of the following grid to organise your notes:

	Overall view of writer	Main points or evidence	Do you agree or not? Why?
Text 1			
Text 2			
Text 3			

English Works

Who's Responsible?

Having decided on your own viewpoint, you are now going to develop your ideas, then explain and justify them to the class. You will be planning a short formal talk lasting three to four minutes on the following issue:

Who should be held responsible in severe cases of truancy and what actions should be taken?

First of all you will need to plan the overall structure of your talk. You must address the two related issues mentioned in the title of your talk: responsibility and action. To be convincing you will need to make a number of clear points and give reasons to support them. You will also have to consider what you will say in the introduction and conclusion of your speech.

Use the following framework as a starting point to help you plan your speech. Using a copy, briefly note key points in each section:

Section 1 – Introduction
Briefly explain the issues and how you intend to address them in your speech

Section 2 – Who should be held responsible?
Consider in turn the responsibility of different parties: for example, pupil, parent or guardian, school, local council. For each one, explain the degree to which they should be held responsible and why

Section 3 – What actions should be taken?
Explain what actions should be taken in cases of severe truancy and why

Section 4 – Concluding comments
Briefly sum up your views, aiming to persuade the audience that you are right!

Report back to the class on how you intend to structure your speech. Improve your plan if necessary.

English Works

When you are happy with your plan, the next stage is to write a detailed version of your speech. Remember this is a formal talk and you need to justify your views to the audience. You are going to need to think carefully about the language you use. The following advice might help you.

TASK

Discuss anything you would add to the following advice.

- **Use Standard English (SE):** To be formal you will need to avoid slang or colloquial expressions so you will not be using sentences like 'All skivers should be grassed up to the old bill'. Use SE instead: 'In severe cases, information about truants should be provided to the local police force'. Remember SE can vary in formality and you do not wish to come across as over-formal.

- **Signal your structure:** Make it easy for your audience to follow your line of thought. Signal when you are moving from one section of your talk to another. Useful phrases could include:
  - *In this talk, I shall...*   – *In the next part of my talk, I...*
  - *To sum up...*   – *Now I want to move on to...*

- **Explain your views clearly:** Use clear, forceful language and avoid long-winded, over complicated sentences. Write in the first person (*I believe...*). You will probably make frequent use of the present tense in making points (Most parents *are* able to...) but past tense when referring to supportive evidence (The judge *was* right to...). You will probably need to use modal verbs such as 'should' when asserting your views (Pupils *should* be able to...).

- **Justify your point of view:** Convince the audience of your viewpoint by using this pattern: explain your point, provide evidence or supportive detail, clinch it. Typical phrases here include:
  - *In my view...* or *It is my belief that...*
  - *I shall now explain why...* or *Support for this is provided by...* or *For instance...* or *I think this because...*
  - *So it is clearly the case that...* or *Thus...*

Now write the detailed version of your speech, referring to your plan.

English Works

Who's Responsible?

① Just before you give your speech, think about what you need to do to maximise its impact on your audience. Think about further suggestions that could be added to those below:

You will now be asked to deliver your speech to the class.

② As you listen to the speeches, take brief notes on the following:
   ❑ The ideas expressed
   ❑ How convinced you are by the viewpoints
   ❑ The use of Standard English
   ❑ How easy it is to follow the argument
   ❑ The quality of the delivery
   ❑ The overall impact

③ Working with a partner, choose two talks that you felt were the most successful and discuss why. Report key points to the rest of the class.

④ Still working with your partner, consider each other's talk. Suggest two things you each might do differently if you had to present your talk again.

English Works

One of the key objectives in this unit is to make a counter-argument to a view that has been expressed. In order to do this, you need to find weaknesses in the argument and offer an alternative point of view that is supported by convincing evidence.

The following letter was sent to the *Banbury Guardian* in response to the newspaper's coverage of the Patricia Amos case. The writer clearly feels little sympathy for Ms Amos.

TASK

1. Read the letter then note five reasons that the writer gives to support her view.
2. Report your reasons to the rest of the class.

Anarchy not to be tolerated

YOUR banner headline, Jail Hell Goes On (*Banbury Guardian*, May 16) regarding Ms Amos's imprisonment was journalistic hyperbole.

Her sentence will probably be spent in the hospital wing and likely to be quashed on appeal within days.

Spare a thought instead for the harassed staff of the education and social services trying to cope with her and her daughters for years on end.

Hell might have more properly described *their* plight!

By spurning all approaches from counsellors with offers of help, Ms Amos is revealed as the architect of her own misfortune and deserving of little sympathy.

The town's magistrates are to be congratulated on their brave stand against this type of two-fingers-up behaviour towards those who are simply trying to help.

Perhaps those with similar attitudes to Ms Amos will now get the message that personal freedom endowed by the democratic process is not a licence to behave exactly as you please with no regard to the law.

Such behaviour represents anarchy, which has no place in civilised society.

An Oxfordshire democrat

You may have noted some of the following:

- Ms Amos is likely to have an easy time in prison
- Ms Amos is unlikely to serve the whole of her sentence
- We should have more sympathy with the education department and social services who tried hard to help Ms Amos
- Ms Amos caused her own problems by refusing offers of help
- The magistrates who sentenced Ms Amos should be praised for their courage
- Other parents may learn a lesson from this case

English Works

Who's Responsible?

TASK

Look more closely at the reasons given by the letter writer to support her point of view. For each one, it is possible to find a weakness and to offer an alternative view. With a partner, discuss the weaknesses in each argument in order to complete a copy of the following chart:

Original argument	Weakness	Alternative view
Ms Amos is likely to have an easy time in prison.		
Ms Amos is unlikely to serve the whole of her sentence.		
We should have more sympathy with the education department and social services who tried hard to help Ms Amos.		
Ms Amos caused her own problems by refusing offers of help.	– Where is the evidence to support this? – How do we know that Ms. Amos received offers of help? – How do we know that she rejected the offers? – Were there reasons why she might not have responded to offers of help?	– Ms Amos says that she did not receive many of the letters which were supposedly sent. – Ms Amos had many problems which she was trying to deal with on her own. – We should sympathise with a single mother struggling to cope with difficult children.
The magistrates who sentenced Ms Amos should be praised for their courage. Other parents may learn a lesson from this case.		

English Works

Look again at the fifth paragraph of the letter. You have already identified weaknesses in this argument but notice how the writer also tries to influence the reader at word and sentence level:

> By **spurning** all approaches from **counsellors** with offers of help, **Ms Amos is revealed** as the **architect of her own misfortune** and deserving of little sympathy.

- *choice of noun suggests kindly people offering help* → counsellors
- *emotive verb* → spurning
- *passive voice = formal tone* → Ms Amos is revealed
- *metaphor designed to blame her entirely* → architect of her own misfortune

Now look at the way a counter-argument can be constructed using similar devices:

> **Struggling to cope** with **difficult personal circumstances**, the **unfortunate** Ms Amos was **clearly** unable to cope with the flood of letters arriving from official departments. **Understandably**, her response was to ignore them in the hope that her problems would disappear. **Surely** the **poor** woman deserves **our sympathy** rather than our condemnation!

- *sentence begins with present participle to suggest she is still struggling* → Struggling to cope
- *noun phrase to emphasise her difficulties* → difficult personal circumstances
- *assertive use of adverbs aimed to sway reader into agreeing with writer's viewpoint* → clearly, Understandably, Surely
- *use of pronoun (our) includes the reader in its assertion* → our sympathy
- *emotive adjectives to gain reader's sympathy* → unfortunate, poor

English Works

Who's Responsible?

TASK

Now write a reply to the newspaper editor in which you counter the arguments in the original letter. Use a copy of the plan below to help you:

Introduction e.g. *Your letter from an Oxfordshire democrat was narrow-minded and intolerant…*
Refute first argument
Refute second argument
Refute third argument e.g. *Struggling to cope with difficult personal circumstances, the unfortunate Ms Amos was clearly unable to cope with the flood of letters arriving from official departments. Understandably, her response was to ignore them in the hope that her problems would disappear. Surely the poor woman deserves our sympathy rather than our condemnation!*
Refute fourth argument
Refute fifth argument
Refute sixth argument
Conclusion

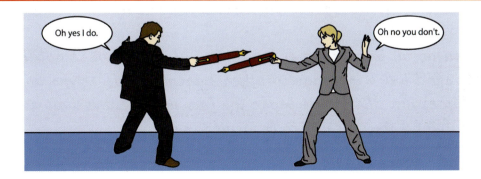

English Works

TASK

Now choose one of the other texts on pages 7 and 8 and write a counter-argument letter in which you identify weaknesses in the original argument and offer an alternative point of view.

Remember to use:
- ❏ An introduction and a conclusion
- ❏ Paragraphs which counter one argument at a time
- ❏ Evidence to support each counter-argument
- ❏ Active or passive voice as appropriate
- ❏ Present tense
- ❏ Words which suggest strong personal conviction e.g. adverbs such as obviously, certainly, surely
- ❏ Emotive vocabulary e.g. poor

82, Priests Drive,
Barnfield,
Essex,
BF3 8GH.
18th July.

The Editor
Dear Sir,
I was shocked to read your editorial about the Patricia Amos case in last week's 'Times Educational Supplement'.

You suggest the public will have been very surprised by her sentence. Frankly, I was far from surprised. This woman had allowed her daughters…

You go on to argue that the jailing of Ms Amos is not the right way to send out a message to other parents. This seems an outrageous suggestion. Ms Amos broke the law in the same way as other criminals and she deserves to be treated in the…

English Works

UNIT 2 On the edge

KEY OBJECTIVES

In this unit you will learn about the following key objectives:

Compare texts – reading short extracts from psychological thrillers to compare how writers use language to create effects

Narrative techniques – experimenting with different ways of writing narrative

Layers of meaning – recognising the subtleties of the word choices writers make and applying these concepts to your own work

Paragraph cohesion – exploring how to link within and between paragraphs so that your writing has coherence and consistency

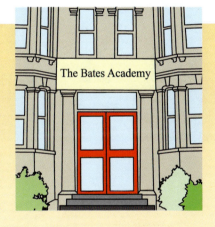

To meet these targets, you are invited to become a student at The Bates Academy of Writing, a college that specialises in the training of 'budding' writers. As up-and-coming writers, you will need to learn your craft, the craft of engaging your readers. The Academy is able to introduce you to a wealth of texts which will demonstrate the many and various methods skilled writers use to manipulate readers into responding emotionally and thinking critically.

You will have the opportunity of attending writing seminars. The genre to be studied this semester is: 'psychological thrillers'.

In order to graduate from The Academy, you will be expected to produce a piece of writing that is of publishable quality.

English Works

Psychological thrillers often make very successful films. Their vivid characters, tension-filled plots and cunning use of narrative techniques, allow film directors to manipulate the emotions of their audiences in much the same way as writers manipulate their readers. This approach, in both films and novels, is often achieved by varying the manner in which we, as readers, perceive the story. For instance, a writer might allow us to see into the mind of a character, so that we can see his or her intentions, or the writer might use more than one narrator, so that the reader perceives the same story from different angles. How we react to these voices, determines our response as readers.

TASK

1. In pairs, take a few moments to list psychological thrillers which have been turned into films e.g. *It* or *The Shining*. Can you name any writers of psychological thrillers? What makes a good writer in this genre? Why?

2. Now report back to the rest of the class.

You are going to be given the challenging task of planning and writing your own psychological thriller. To do so, you will need to behave like a writer. Writers continuously jot down thoughts and ideas throughout the writing process. This is how you need to begin your writing.

English Works

On the edge

Here is an example of a jotter page that you will be expected to keep during your time at The Academy.

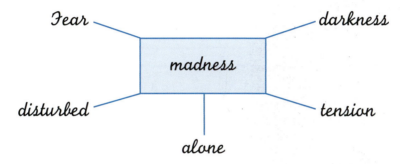

This jotter page includes some words we might associate with madness.

TASK

Start your own jotter by adding words which link with this theme. Try consulting a thesaurus or dictionary to build up a variety of synonyms.

Psychological thrillers always focus on both the **conscious** and **subconscious parts** of the brain. The conscious mind is the part of the brain which we are aware of. It controls our everyday thoughts and actions. However, the subconscious mind can sometimes come to the fore. The subconscious mind often protects the conscious mind from strong emotions by storing them away from everyday concerns. The tension between the conscious and subconscious mind (between what we feel we should do and what we might do) provides fertile ground for writers.

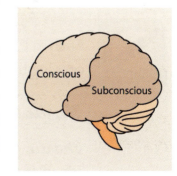

English Works

Opening the mind

To write a good psychological thriller you will need to have the imagination to climb inside the mind of your characters. You also need the skills of a psychologist so that you can explore the conscious and the subconscious.

TASK

Read the following extracts from *Flowers for Algernon* by **Daniel Keyes**. They are about a character called Charlie who has had a recent operation. Charlie is struggling to come to terms with the internal conflict between his conscious and subconscious mind. The narrative style reflects how the character speaks.

I told Dr Strauss what good is it to get smart in my sleep. I want to be smart when I'm awake. He says it's the same thing and I have two minds. There's the *subconscious* and the *conscious* (that's how you spell it.) And one don't tell the other one what its doing. They don't even talk to each other. That's why I dream. And boy I been having crazy dreams. Wow. Ever since that night T.V. The late late late late show. I forgot to ask him if it was only me or if everybody had those two minds.

(I just looked up the word in the dictionary Dr Strauss gave me. *The word subconscious. Adj. Of the nature of mental operations yet not present in consciousness, as: subconscious conflict of desires.*) Theres more but I still don't know what it means This isn't a very good dictionary for dumb people like me.

I have often reread my progress reports and seen the illiteracy. The childish nairvete, the mind of low intelligence peering from a dark room, through the keyhole, at the dazzling light outside. I see that even in my dullness I knew that I was inferior, and that other people has something I lacked – something denied me. In my mental blindness, I thought that it was somehow connected with the ability to read and write, and I was sure that if I could get those skills I would automatically have intelligence too.

TASK

Analyse Charlie's state of mind. Give evidence to support your view by copying the grid below on to a page in your jotter and completing it.

Charlie's state of mind	Evidence
Charlie feels secure and safe about the experiment.	'It's good to be smart.'

English Works

On the edge

Experiencing voices

Writers consider very carefully whose viewpoint they use to narrate a story. They do this by using either the first, second or third person.

Look at the diagrams below to remind yourself of the first and third person types of narration.

We only know what the character wants…

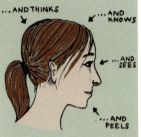

First person

❙❙ We are alone on the island now, Barney and I. It was something of a jolt to have to sack Tayloe after all these years, but I had no alternative. (*Barney* by Will Stanton) ❙❙

The writer can tell us what to think about characters and their actions. We can see…

Third person

❙❙ Green material is simply impossible to work with. Much experimentation went into this, along with much heartbreak before Mr Gumb got it right. (*Silence of the Lambs* by Thomas Harris) ❙❙

After reading the extracts above, answer the following questions:

1. By using the first person in *Barney*, the character talks directly to us. What do we learn about this character through first person narration?
2. In the Thomas Harris text, the narrator is referring to Mr Gumb. What does he tell us about this character? How do we know the narrator is telling us the truth?

Use of the second person in narrative is rare. It is a style more suited to instruction manuals, walking tour guides and recipes. The second person uses 'you' and is, therefore, a very direct style.

TASK

Writing changes its effectiveness depending on whether it is written in the first or third person.

Read the extract below. The pronouns and verbs have been underlined. Rewrite the extract on a page in your jotter and change the text from first person to third person. For instance, you would begin with, 'She lay there on that great…'. (N.B. You may have to make other minor changes to keep the sense of the passage.)

> <u>I lie</u> here on this great immovable bed – it is nailed down, <u>I believe</u> – and <u>follow</u> that pattern about by the hour. It is as good as gymnastics, <u>I assure</u> you. <u>I start</u>, <u>we'll</u> say, at the bottom, down in the corner over there where it has not been touched, and <u>I determine</u> for the thousandth time that <u>I will follow</u> that pointless pattern to some sort of a conclusion.
>
> **(The Yellow Wall Paper** by Charlotte Perkins Gilman)

TASK

❶ Discuss the following questions:
   • Which of the versions do you prefer?
   • Does each version still work for you as a reader?
   • Which has more impact on you?
   • Why is one more effective than the other?

❷ Using a page in your jotter, choose three sentences you find particularly interesting, either third person or first person, from the text above, and write them down for future reference. Keeping notes in this way will help you to build up a store of ideas for your own psychological thriller.

English Works

Questions of the mind

The most important part of any story has to be the opening. This is when the reader is hooked. As trainees, it is necessary for you to develop this skill now.

Read the following two openings. What questions come to mind when you read the passages for the first time? What intrigues you as a reader? Jot down the words the writers use to create atmosphere and any other ways you think the reader is hooked.

TRUE! – nervous – very, very dreadfully nervous I had been and am; but why will you say that I am mad? The disease had sharpened my senses – not destroyed – not dulled them. Above all was the sense of hearing acute. I heard all things in the heaven and in the earth. I heard many things in hell. How, then, am I mad? Harken! and observe how healthily – how calmly I can tell you the whole story.

(*The Tell-Tale Heart* by **Edgar Allan Poe**)

Dr Strauss showed me how to keep the TV turned low so now I can sleep. I dont hear a thing. And still don't understand what it says. A few times I play it over in the morning to find out what I lerned when I was sleeping and I don't think so. Miss Kinnian says Maybe its another langwidge or something. But most times it sounds American. It talks so fast faster than even Miss Gold who was my teacher in 6 grade and I remember she talked so fast I couldn't understand her.

(*Flowers for Algernon* by **Daniel Keyes**)

Discuss with three or four other trainees which of the following words you would use to describe the narrator of each of the above extracts, and why.

A thrilling story

It is always exciting to experiment with the opening to a story, as there are so many ways to begin. What are the essential points for an effective opening? An effective opening should:

- Provide a moment which will hook the reader – perhaps a description of a shocking event or a slice of wicked conversation
- Provide only some of the answers. The reader must be made to think; to speculate; to worry; to predict
- Use vocabulary appropriate to the style – for instance, a Gothic horror tale might use words such as 'gloomy', 'storm', 'morose', or 'eerie'

1. Before you begin writing, spend time noting down your initial ideas.
2. Then, write an opening for your own psychological thriller. For example:

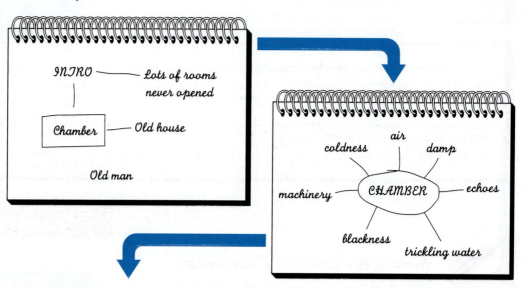

There were rooms in the farthest corners, rooms from other lives that hadn't been opened in years. Beyond them was a chamber that was black to human vision, but full of small sounds. Water trickles here and small pumps hum.

3. Swap your opening paragraphs with a partner. Read each other's and note down any words or phrases which seem effective. Discuss these with your partner.

English Works

On the edge

Journeys through the mind

In addition to openings, characters are also a major consideration for a writer. They need to appear realistic in order to make the reader believe in them, yet they also need to have some unique qualities that make them both attractive and interesting.

Read the second paragraph of *The Tell-Tale Heart* given below. Read this passage closely. What can you deduce about the behaviour and mental state of the character? Discuss your findings with a partner.

> It is impossible to say how first the idea entered my brain; but once conceived, it haunted me day and night. Object there was none. Passion there was none. I loved the old man. He had never wronged me. He had never given me insult. For his gold I had no desire. I think it was his eye! yes, it was this! He had the eye of a vulture – a pale blue eye, with film over it. Whenever it fell upon me, my blood ran cold; and so by degrees – very gradually – I made up my mind to take the life of the old man, and thus rid myself of the eye forever.

Working as a small group, use a jotter page and create a psychological profile for an imaginary character. There is an example here.

English Works 25

Now that you have created your unique character, he or she needs to come alive in your writing. This can be done through a careful choice of vocabulary, sentence structure, punctuation and detail.

TASK

1. Challenge another group of trainees to bring your character to life by swapping your profile with them. Working as a group, ask them to write a paragraph describing a character based on your profile. They can choose whether they write in the first or third person.

2. Once completed, read through their paragraph and discuss your responses. Does it match your profile? How have they used language to create the character?

TASK

Now write your own character profile and accompanying paragraph. You are at the stage where you should feel confident to do this. You may wish to use the paragraph you have already created in your story.

English Works

On the edge

The told and the untold

Language is power. Politicians use it, advertisers use it, lawyers use it and writers use it to manipulate the reactions of their audience. One way they do this is by deciding on the form of writing they will use and controlling the order and choice of words.

Read the police record sheet below which records an incident. The information states the actions of the accused in a factual way.

Newland Constabulary

Police Record Sheet

Accused	Lee Tate
Age	48
Occupation	Unemployed (previously employed by *Go Far Bus Company Ltd*)
Crime Committed	Disturbance of peace

Brief details of event

On the 27th of April Mr Tate entered the *CCD Broadcasting* building at approximately 10.30am. He made his way to the main broadcasting suite, shouting loudly and incoherently at 'Derek Disco' during the 'Melting Moments' slot for the over 60s.

Mr Tate took advantage of the fact that 'Derek Disco' was out of his seat calling for security and announced on air that the *Go Far Bus Company* was unsafe and that listeners should not use it.

Extra details

Go Far Bus Company are currently suing Mr Tate for slander. Case pending.

Crow prosecuting on behalf of *CCD Broadcasting* for trespassing, disturbing the peace and corrupting the airwaves. Case pending.

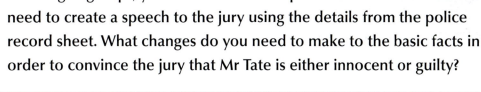

Working in groups, you will either be the prosecution or the defence. You need to create a speech to the jury using the details from the police record sheet. What changes do you need to make to the basic facts in order to convince the jury that Mr Tate is either innocent or guilty?

English Works 27

Now this is the point. You fancy me mad. Madmen know nothing. But you should have seen me. You should have seen how wisely I proceeded – with what caution – with what foresight – with what dissimulation I went to work! I was never kinder to that old man than during the whole week before I killed him. And every night, about midnight, I turned the latch of the door and opened it – oh so gently! And then, When I had made an opening sufficient for my head, I put in a dark lantern, all closed, closed, that no light shone out, and then I thrust in my head. Oh, you would have laughed to see how cunningly I thrust it in! I moved it slowly – very, very slowly, so that I might not disturb the old man's sleep. It took me an hour to place my whole head within the opening so far that I could see him as he lay upon his bed. Ha! Would a madman have been so wise as this, And then, when my head was well in the room, I undid the lantern cautiously – oh, so cautiously – cautiously (for the hinges creaked) – I undid it just so much that a single ray of light fell upon the vulture eye. And this I did for seven long nights – every night just at midnight – but I found the eye always closed; and so it was impossible to do the work; for it was not the old man who vexed me, but his Evil Eye. And every morning, when the day broke, I went boldly into the chamber, and spoke courageously to him, calling him by name in a hearty tone, and enquiring how he has passed the night. So you see he would have been a very profound old man, indeed, to suspect that every night, just at twelve, I looked on him while he slept.

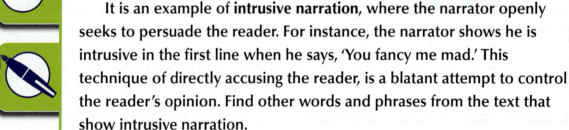

Now read the third paragraph of *The Tell-Tale Heart* above.

It is an example of **intrusive narration**, where the narrator openly seeks to persuade the reader. For instance, the narrator shows he is intrusive in the first line when he says, 'You fancy me mad.' This technique of directly accusing the reader, is a blatant attempt to control the reader's opinion. Find other words and phrases from the text that show intrusive narration.

Omniscient narration is crucially different from intrusive narration. It involves an 'all knowing' narrator. A writer will usually use the third person for omniscient narration to control the reader's response by shaping it e.g. the narrator in *The Silence of the Lambs*.

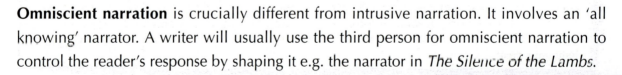

❶ Using *omniscient* narration, work with a partner to write a sentence describing a character waking up in a hospital bed.
❷ Repeat the task but this time use *intrusive* narration.
❸ Discuss which you think is more effective and why.

English Works

Multiple narration

Have you ever seen a film or read a story where whoever is telling the story keeps changing? Multiple narration is where more than one character narrates the story. This can be dramatic and enticing.

TASK

There are two narrators in the following extracts from Robert Swindell's *Stone Cold*. Working with a partner, try to identify the two narrative voices. Which extract belongs to which narrative voice?

> You can call me Link. It's not my name, but it's what I say when anybody asks, which isn't often. I'm invisible, see? One of the invisible people. Right now I'm sitting in the doorway watching the passers-by. They avoid looking at me. They're afraid I want something they've got, and they're right. Hang about and I'll tell you the story of my fascinating life.

> Shelter. Yes. I like it. It's got a ring to it as I'm sure you'll agree. Shelter, as in shelter from the stormy blast. It's what they're all seeking. The street people. What they crave. If they can only find shelter everything will be fine. Well – get fell in, my lucky lads. I'm ready for you.

> It has happened again. I was on my way to inspect theatreland when two dossers approached me. One – the scruffier of the two – asked me for change. I responded in my usual way, and as I passed on I distinctly heard them laughing. I hope for their sakes that they manage to retain that sense of humour because they'll need it quite soon.

> Fella rang my bell last night. 22.00 hours. I wasn't worried. Provided you've got the situation under control there's nothing to worry about. A swift recce through the curtain showed me a shortish chap of about forty-five. It was too dark for me to see his features but something about the way he was standing told me he was agitated so I judged it best not to reveal my position. I never show a strong light after dusk.

> I hardly slept at all. Thoughts whirled round and round inside my skull and I was as hungry as hell. There were loads of parked cars on Pratt Street and people kept coming past, chatting and laughing, banging doors and revving up. I was glad when it had started to come light.

> The strength of the insane. I'd come across that phrase, and now I found out what it meant. I'm not a small guy and he was a lot older but I couldn't break free. I'd bucked and writhed and lashed out with my feet, he wrapped his arms around me and his grip was like bands of steel. My feet left the floor and he carried me across the room like he'd carried the cat, except he didn't croon or nuzzle, and when we reached the hole in the floor he threw me down and fell on me like a wrestler.

English Works

TASK

Here are two more extracts from the same book featuring the two narrators. Compare their language. It reveals two very different characters. Look particularly at the way they each use specific sorts of vocabulary, sentence length and grammar. Copy the comparison box on to a page in your jotter to help to organise your responses.

> Laughing boy one. That was the codename of the exercise. It was meticulously planned and beautifully executed, and now it's time for de-briefing. In a well-regulated army, every operation was followed by a thorough de-briefing. A sort of inquest, if you'll pardon the grisly joke. So.

> We were a family, you know – as happy as most, till dad ran off with the receptionist in 1991, when I was fourteen and at the local comp. This mucked up my school work for a while, but that's not why I ended up like this. No. Vincent's to blame for that. Good old Vince. Mum's boyfriend. You should see him. I mean, Mum's no Kylie Minogue – but Vincent. He's about fifty for a start, and he's one of these old dudes that wear cool gear and try to act young and it doesn't work because they've got grey hair and fat bellies and they just make themselves pathetic.

	Narrator A	Narrator B
Specific vocabulary	Uses military words such as codename	
Sentence type		Lots of short sentences suggesting informality and, yet, quite emphatic e.g. 'Mum's boyfriend'
Tone	Seems to be quite sarcastic e.g. 'Laughing boy'	
Grammar		A younger voice comes through because many sentences are compound (overuse of 'and')

TASK

1. Discuss with a partner what you find effective in these extracts. What are the hooks for you as readers and which aspects of language (words, images, phrases, dialogue) do you find appealing. Explain your reasons.
2. Write two paragraphs of your narrative on a page in your jotter. Experiment with this technique by using two characters to narrate the same event.

English Works

On the edge

A chilling story

Deciding what goes where in a story is vital to what extent your audience both understands and enjoys what they are reading. Some stories stick to a traditional format which makes the reader feel comfortable as they know what is likely to happen next. Other stories adopt a more varied structure which can engross, surprise and delight the reader. For example, some novels actually begin with a dramatic ending and the reader's job is to work out why such an ending occurred.

TASK

❶ Below are some key events from a psychological thriller. Work in a group and re-arrange the order of the events to come up with three separate stories.

- Man goes home to find that his house has been burgled
- A theft takes place
- Man is being persuaded by police to climb down from top of building
- An ambulance siren is heard in the distance
- Police officer drives at full speed through town
- Man hears voices telling him to catch a criminal

❷ Compare your versions with other groups. Which do you think will be the most gripping? Why?

❸ Discuss what different narrative voices you could include in these versions to provide the reader with different insights on the events or different perspectives.

English Works

The journey begins

You should already have the basic outline of your plot written on your jotter page and your main characters should be clearly defined. The time has come for you to write your opening! Without looking back in the book, try to remember three key features of effective openings.

TASK

❶ Choose what type of opening you would like to use. Remember, the opening lines must shock or intrigue your reader. You must employ a 'hook'. Try it out orally by first working with a partner. Check that your partner has the response you intended:
   ❑ What impact did you make?
   ❑ Were they intrigued?
   ❑ Did you keep them guessing?
   ❑ Could they make a prediction?
   ❑ How could you improve it?
❷ Now write the first paragraph of your thriller.

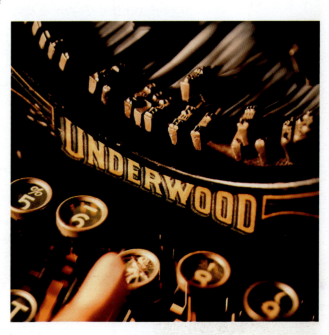

TASK

Once you have completed your opening, show it to a fellow trainee and discuss the decisions you have made. He or she may offer you an idea for an alternative way to open your story. If so, discuss the variations and your preferences.

English Works

Beginnings and endings

It may seem bizarre to think about endings when you have just worked on your beginning. However, links *do* need to be made so that your story makes sense.

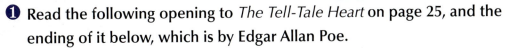

TASK

1. Read the following opening to *The Tell-Tale Heart* on page 25, and the ending of it below, which is by Edgar Allan Poe.
2. Discuss what links you can make between the two extracts. Use these further questions to guide your thinking:
   - Who is narrating the story?
   - Where do you think they might be?
   - How much time might have elapsed between the opening line and the last line?
   - What is going on?
   - Why does the narrator end with this line? What does it suggest that he has done?

I swung the chair upon which I had been sitting, and grated it upon the boards, but the noise arose over all and continually increased. It grew louder – louder – louder! And still the men chatted pleasantly, and smiled. Was it possible they heard not? Almighty God! – no, no! They heard! – they suspected! – they knew! – they were making a mockery of my horror! – this I thought, and this I think. But anything was better than this agony! Anything was more tolerable than this derision! I could bear those hypocritical smiles no longer! I felt that I must scream or die! And now – again! – hark! louder! louder! louder! louder! "Villains!" I shrieked, "dissemble no more! I admit the deed! – tear up the planks! Here, here! – It is the beating of his hideous heart!"

TASK

Keep your opening in mind and write an ending making as many links to the start as possible. When you have finished, show another trainee your work and ask them to point out anything you have included in the opening that hasn't been resolved in the ending.

Tense moments

When we read stories, there are moments which make our pulses race faster because, as readers, we are responding to the tension of a situation. This tension is created by writers through a combination of conflict and timing and it is supported by punctuation which influences the pace of our reading and the dramatic effect.

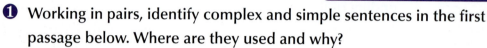

1. Working in pairs, identify complex and simple sentences in the first passage below. Where are they used and why?
2. Now read the other passages. How is the tension created? Use a copy to text mark them and look particularly at the sentence length and the use of punctuation. What other techniques have been used to create tension?

Upon the eighth night I was more than usually cautious in opening the door. A watch's minute hand moves more quickly than did mine. Never before that night had I felt the extent of my own powers – of my sagacity. I could scarcely contain my feelings of triumph. To think that there I was, opening the door, little by little, and he not even to dream of my secret deeds or thoughts. I fairly chuckled at the idea; and perhaps he heard me; for he moved on the bed suddenly, as of startled. Now you may think that I drew back – but no. His room was as black as pitch with the thick darkness, (for the shutters were close fastened, through fear of robbers,) and so I knew that he could not see the opening of the door, and I kept pushing it on steadily, steadily.

I had my head in, and was about to open the lantern, when my thumb slipped upon the tin fastening, and the old man sprang up in bed, crying out – "who's there?" I kept quite still and said nothing. For a whole hour I did not move a muscle.

Presently I heard a slight groan, and I knew it was the groan of mortal terror. It was not a groan of pain or of grief – oh, no! – it was the low stifled sound that arises from the bottom of the soul when overcharged with awe. I knew the sound well.

Look closely at your own narrative writing. In small groups, discuss how you can introduce elements of tension to your work by considering sentence length and punctuation.

English Works

On the edge

Seeing, not saying

Writers like to take control. They attempt to make sure that the reader can only see what the writer wants them to see. This can be achieved by providing a very unusual view of everyday events or items. To achieve this effect, writers have to use specific, vivid and detailed description, which can often be very lyrical. In the poem below, the poet wants us, as readers, to view everyday objects as if we had never seen them before.

TASK

1. In pairs read through the 'postcard' below and see if you can work out which everyday objects the Martian finds on Earth.
2. Look back over your ideas so far and see if you can add some examples like this which force the reader to think about everyday objects in a new and unusual way.

A Martian Sends A Postcard Home

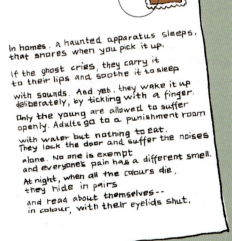

Caxtons are mechanical birds with many wings
and some are treasured for their markings--

they cause the eyes to melt
or the body to shriek without pain.

I have never seen one fly, but
sometimes they perch on the hand.

Mist is when the sky is tired of flight
and rests its soft machine on ground:

then the world is dim and bookish
like engravings under tissue paper.

Rain is when the earth is television.
It has the properties of making colours darker.

Model T is a room with the lock inside--
a key is turned to free the world

for movement, so quick there is a film
to watch for anything missed.

But time is tied to the wrist
or kept in a box, ticking with impatience.

In homes, a haunted apparatus sleeps,
that snores when you pick it up.

If the ghost cries, they carry it
to their lips and soothe it to sleep

with sounds. And yet, they wake it up
deliberately, by tickling with a finger.

Only the young are allowed to suffer
openly. Adults go to a punishment room

with water but nothing to eat.
They lock the door and suffer the noises

alone. No one is exempt
and everyone's pain has a different smell.

At night, when all the colours die,
they hide in pairs

and read about themselves--
in colour, with their eyelids shut.

English Works 35

As trainees, you need a really good way of practising describing objects, people or places in detail. An interesting technique is to **ban** using any names. When you ban a word you need to make a quick brainstorm of all the words you would associate with the thing you are describing. See the examples below.

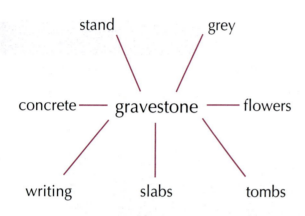

'The gravestone stood in the cemetery'

'The slanted concrete slabs stood stoically whilst the wild roses entwined covering names of lost loved ones.'

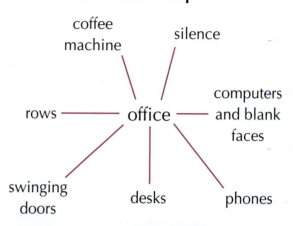

'The office was quiet'

'Behind the swinging doors by rows of blank faces, the phones are sleeping, exhausted from the conversations of the day.'

TASK

❶ To enhance your writing, create a sentence describing the nouns below without using the word.

rain **laughter** **shoe**
mist **radio** **fork**

❷ Now choose at least 3 sentences from your own story. Ban specific words and re-draft using more detail.

Webs of the mind

To impress and entertain your readers you need to use sophisticated and precise vocabulary. One way to do this is to use word webs. Word webs help a writer to think of alternatives for a word. This makes sure that words are varied and interesting. By looking at the alternatives in the word web, a writer is able to choose which is the most appropriate for their sentence.

TASK

1. Below is an example of a word web. Copy it on to a page of your jotter and add as many more as you can.

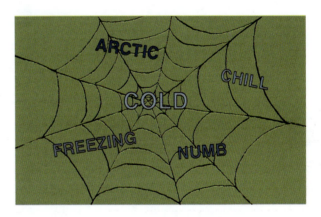

2. Have a go at creating your own word webs with words that are associated with psychological thrillers. For example, fear, looked, loud or big.
3. Read back through your story and select words which you feel you can improve on. Create a word web to help you decide on an alternative. Then continue with your story and include some of your word web ideas.

WARNING!

Make sure your writing is balanced! Sophisticated vocabulary is good, but be careful – too much distracts from the overall enjoyment!

Ask the experts

We always need help and advice from experts. As trainees you are all gifted in different areas. For example, one trainee may have an excellent creative imagination whereas another trainee may excel in using effective and accurate punctuation. Each skill is as important as the other and both will add value to a story.

TASK

Working in pairs, consider what elements make a good story. Make a quick list. Report back your answers to the whole class.

TASK

As a class you need to divide yourselves into groups, each group will be a 'table of expertise'. Fellow trainees can then consult the different groups about their work. The tables of expertise could be…

Look at your story and identify which expert you would like to consult for help. Remember that as an expert in your field you will be called on to help another trainee. As you are waiting for your turn, continue with your story.

English Works

On the edge

Video diary

Your stories are now complete and provided you've followed each of the seminars carefully, you should be nearing graduation.

TASK

❶ Read through your completed story and choose a favourite moment and a technique you feel you've really worked on successfully. For example, you may feel that you've used punctuation to achieve a particularly good effect.

I chose to use a complex sentence here to help build up an image in the reader's mind

I've done that well!

This is great!

Wow! My vocabulary is good here

Look how I used punctuation to create that effect!

That sounds really professional!

❷ Now read your chosen extracts to your fellow trainees, explaining the techniques you've used and the reasons for the choices you have made.

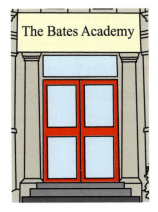

English Works

Edge of the precipice

> All good writing is swimming under water and holding your breath. (F. Scott Fitzgerald)

In pairs discuss the above quotation. What do you think the metaphor of swimming under water might mean? How is swimming under water similar to writing? What was F. Scott Fitzgerald referring to here?

As trainees of The Academy it is time to leave your mark!

TASK

On a jotter page, draw around your hand. Inside the line create your own metaphor or simile describing **your** experience of writing your own story. Try to come up with something original. You could use a quote from any of the extracts in this unit.

The time has come for you to hand in your story for publication.

Congratulations!

You have successfully graduated from The Bates Academy of Writing, passing the psychological thriller narrative writing course with honours.

Signed…. *G. Rollerson*

Principal

English Works

UNIT 3 Testing times

KEY OBJECTIVES

In this unit you will learn about the following key objectives:

Degrees of formality – writing in ways appropriate to your audience and purpose

Sustained Standard English – securing your ability to write effectively for a range of purposes, including formal English

Exploit conventions – understanding and using a range of text types in your writing

Rhetorical devices – reading and responding to a range of different texts in order to identify and explain how writers achieve their effects, including commenting on the language they use

Paragraph organisation – practising planning and writing under timed conditions, both short and extended pieces

Narrative techniques – writing an action narrative

This unit will help you to prepare for the end of key stage 3 tests in English. Interestingly, the texts you will be reading all have one thing in common: they are based on the written experiences of people, past and present, under extreme pressure in difficult circumstances!

English Works 41

What, where, when and why?

TASK

Have a look at the following short extracts. Use the clues in the texts to see if you can identify:

- ❏ What kind of text it is. What tells you this?
- ❏ Where it might have appeared
- ❏ When it might have been written
- ❏ Why it was written – its purpose
- ❏ Whether you get any clues about the writer

1. Very soon, she will smell the land. Two hundred miles out from these ancient French sands, somewhere under a bruised sky growing lower and grimmer by the second, Ellen MacArthur is almost home; hanging on desperately, with a mast likely to crash down in seconds if her luck finally deserts her, but almost home.

2. 'It was amazing,' says Dr David Pemberton, Senior Curator of Zoology at Tasmanian Museum and Art Gallery, who rushed to the scene just in time to save the delicate corpse from the incoming tide and is now making arrangements for it to be analysed and put on public display.

3. Now available in DVD and VHS we are pleased to offer the Collector's Edition of **SHACKLETON**.

4. One of the sailors, posted on the top ladderstep, unscrewed the bolts of the panels. But hardly were the screws loosed, when the panel rose with great violence, evidently drawn by the suckers of a poulp's arm.

5. I awoke with a start from a short nap. I looked out of the window in the cabin and there it was – an iceberg right by the boat. Within seconds I was on deck, and we passed within 15 to 20 metres of the berg, actually sailing through the white water next to it. All I could think of was what would have happened if we had hit it.

6. All squid belong to the phylum Mollusca, placing them as close relatives to animals like clams and snails. More specifically squid belong to a group of molluscs called cephalopods (meaning head-foot).

Now check the answers. You will find them at the end of the unit.

English Works

Masterclass

The following are some features of the text types used in the extracts opposite:

Recount/Narrative: Purpose – to retell events

Text	Sentence	Word
Usually chronological Paragraphs linked in wide variety of ways	Past tense Active voice Variety of sentence structures to create create effects Dialogue used to show character or move plot forward	Adjectives and adverbs used to create detailed descriptions Imagery – similes and metaphors

Explanation: Purpose – to explain a process or how something works

Text	Sentence	Word
General statement to introduce topic, followed by a series of steps Summary statement to conclude Often accompanied by diagrams diagrams and illustrations	Third person Present tense for phenomena still in existence; past tense for past events Connectives to indicate sequence e.g. *first, next, gradually* or cause cause and effect e.g. *because*	Specialist terminology Impersonal language Mainly nouns and verbs

Report/Information: Purpose – to describe the way things are

Text	Sentence	Word
Opening general statement Organised according to different aspects of the information Information often classified or categorised Use made of different fonts, page-layout allows reader to read in different ways	Third person Present tense Combination of active and passive voice Simple and compound sentences for clarity Connectives emphasise cause and effect and comparison e.g. *then, so, similarly*	Technical terms related to subject Impersonal language Mainly nouns and verbs

Persuasion: Purpose – to argue a case or persuade others to do/believe something

Text	Sentence	Word
Wide range of forms, from adverts to letters, essays etc. Often mixes information (report) with persuasion Thesis (opening statement) followed by elaboration, illustration/evidence and summary Use of different fonts and print sizes for impact	Advertising often uses second person in direct address to reader Active voice Variety of sentence types (questions, statements, exclamations and commands) Formal argument uses connectives to emphasise logic e.g. *therefore, thus* Adverts often subvert formal language for effect	Value judgement words to influence the reader e.g. *clearly, obviously* Adjectives and adverbs for effect Wordplay and imagery

Effective writing often mixes these different text types for specific effects.

Alone, alone, on a wide, wide sea

In February 2001, British yachtswoman Ellen MacArthur took part in the Vendée Globe single-handed race in the yacht 'Kingfisher'. During the race, she regularly sent an email log detailing 95 days of supreme physical effort, cheating death in an icy ocean and battling sleep deprivation before she sailed into port to end her single-handed adventure. Here are three short extracts from her log.

Day 1 Sunday February 11, 2001
It was pretty amazing for me – the emotion of leaving the dock and seeing all the people wave me off down the channel. It finally hit me during the night as I was working on the computer: this is it – I'm doing the Vendée Globe. It hadn't really sunk in until then. So I'd better get on with it...

Day 4
Steep, savage seas, with 45-knot blasts right on the Cape of NW Spain. Last night was the toughest I've spent on board. The wind went from 15 to 45 knots in 30 seconds. The seas were just horrific, I couldn't stop her leaping over each wave and crashing down on to the next. At one point, the carbon shelving on which the stores are stacked collapsed. Very tired.

Day 30
Icebergs – a close call for Kingfisher. I awoke with a start from a short nap. I looked out of the window in the cabin and there it was – an iceberg right by the boat. Within seconds I was on deck, and we passed within 15 to 20 metres of the berg, actually sailing through the white water next to it. All I could think of was what would have happened if we had hit it. The radar was alarmed, but as is sometimes the case, this berg was invisible to it, even when I was right next to it.

TASK

1. What features tell you that this is a log or diary? One has been selected for you: 'Very tired.' A common feature of diaries is the use of **minor** or incomplete sentences. This is a minor sentence because it doesn't have a finite verb. Compare with: 'I awoke with a start from a short nap.' Can you find any other examples of minor sentences in the text above?

2. Find three other examples which illustrate characteristic features of a diary or log. Explain the features you have selected.

Now read on. Opposite is a longer log entry.

English Works

Testing times

Day 56

Never in my life before have I experienced such beauty, and fear at the same time – 10 icebergs so far today. They have ranged from 200 ft in length, to about half a mile. The first was not a surprise, the second neither really – but when the third, fourth, fifth and sixth all appeared in a line with just a mile between them I was bewildered at their frequency. I wanted to gybe north, but ended up hand steering to pass three of the bergs to windward. I gybed between the fifth and sixth only to see the next two – the seventh being the most enormous of all…

I was forced to hand steer to pass the seventh. It was enormous, and for a while I didn't think we'd make it to windward as the wind rose to 30 knots. We made it and I was then faced with the most beautiful iceberg I could imagine. Wide, blue, high-arched caves, and a height that must have been similar to the white cliffs of Dover. So quiet, apart from the waves breaking about its base. High faces of pure white harshly disfigured by deep blue cracks roughly cut from above.

Every 10 minutes I stick my head out and look. Every time I dodge the flying freezing spray – squinting at the horizon till my eyes sting with the cold. I'd just made a cup of tea to try to thaw out when I thought I'd have a last check. Of course there was a berg – stayed up there for half an hour… freezing cold, but eyes glued to the water for growlers (small pieces of ice that break off the main berg). Several times, despite trying to duck, the visor of my jacket is pounded by the waves. Frozen eyelids again.

gybe: to turn the boat

TASK

A log such as Ellen MacArthur's can serve a variety of purposes. Read the entry above again closely, and then, following discussion, complete a copy of the grid below:

Purpose	Example
To record key information	
	Frozen eyelids again.
	High faces of pure white harshly disfigured by deep blue cracks
To communicate the drama of the voyage	

English Works

Now read on:

> After a time going slow without the halyard, Kingfisher is back on track and Ellen finally passes Cape Horn at the southernmost tip of South America two days and 17 hours inside Christophe Auguin's record pace from the 1996 event – and just over two days behind the race leader Michel Desjoyeaux.

Day 66

I feel overwhelmed. The stress and difficulties of the last few days seem to be melting into emotion as I approach the Horn. The second time for Kingfisher and me together. It's a great symbol for the two of us personally, as the very first time I was ever alone on her, was just a few miles from this famous rock.

I cannot help but feel moved deep inside. The thoughts of the past storms and struggles are far off at this point. This race has been hard, but when I think of those here hundreds of years ago I feel very humble sitting here in my hi-tech wet-weather kit. For them, the corner was literally life or death. My heart goes out to all those who have struggled, survived and died on this piece of water.

It's been a long haul since the launch in NZ, and the most incredible adventure of my life. It's far more than just the story of a girl alone at sea. For me it's a story of teamwork, friendship and love. The story of so many people working towards a goal, and if not working, willing us on… I feel there are so many others with me on board. I've never been lonely – far from it.

Source of extracts: *Guardian Unlimited* © Guardian Newspapers Limited 2002

TASK

1. What is different about this log entry? How is Ellen using the log here?
2. She says 'I've never been lonely – far from it.' Why do you think this is so? See if you can find evidence from the earlier entries to support the fact that, despite being literally 'alone, alone on a wide, wide sea', Ellen didn't feel lonely.
3. From your reading of the log entries, what picture of Ellen MacArthur, the person, do you build up? Make a short list using a copy of the following grid:

Achievements and skills	Personal qualities

English Works

Testing times

Now read the following newspaper article, which announced Ellen MacArthur's arrival in second place at the end of the round-the-world race.

It has been divided into two sections, with some reading tasks at the end of each.

Euan Ferguson in Les Sables D'Olonne watches as France prepares to welcome Ellen MacArthur, the British sailor who has become the century's first true heroine.

Very soon, she will smell the land. **Two hundred miles out from these ancient French sands, somewhere under a bruised sky growing lower and grimmer by the second**, Ellen MacArthur is almost home; **hanging on desperately, with a mast likely to crash down in seconds if her luck finally deserts her**, but almost home.

So soon, some time this Sunday morning, she will smell the land; **and then** she will see the boats, **and** the helicopters, **and** the tens of thousands lining the harbour **and** the sands, **and** the most remarkable piece of sailing by a British woman will be over.

She hasn't won the Vendée Globe. That honour, and Ellen's radioed congratulations yesterday, went to Frenchman Michel Desjoyeaux, 'The Professor', who was last night due to sail his yacht PRB, the mouse to whom Ellen has been cat for the last exhilarating fortnight, into port as a filthily wet Les Sables lit up in his honour. He, as has Ellen, has rewritten the record books, sailing round the world single-handed in an astonishing 95 days, tearing the previous time down by 10 days.

TASK

Investigate

❶ Read the first two paragraphs again. Can you write down the **basic information** they convey in a single sentence or two?
That probably wasn't too difficult, because most of the text in these two opening paragraphs provides additional information and detail in the form of **adverbials**. These have been highlighted in green above.

❷ What do you notice about where the adverbials tend to be positioned within the sentences?

❸ The second paragraph is in fact a single sentence. What **effect** does stringing together all the clauses with the conjunction **and** have?

English Works

Masterclass

Using adverbials

Writers often use a simple **adverb** to add information to a verb, an adjective, or even sometimes a whole sentence, for example:

I ***really hated*** the main course (adverb + verb)

The garden is ***really* attractive** (adverb + adjective)

***Seriously*, I think you should work harder** (adverb + sentence)

You can also use **adverbial phrases** – a group of words that function in the same way as an adverb. These are often used to tell the reader where, when or how the action happened, for example:

At around 3pm, the boat sank *quickly, without trace, in mid-ocean*.

when   *how*   *where*

The clever thing about adverbials is that they can often be used in different places in a sentence, for specific effects. Try moving the adverbials above around to see what effects you can create.

Good writers often introduce an event by starting a sentence with an adverbial phrase in order to create tension. It's an almost instant way of improving your writing of narratives and recounts. Try it and see!

Quietly, almost without breathing, she pushed open the door and entered the room

Suddenly, without any warning, the window slammed shut.

English Works

Now read on:

It was exhaustion, finally, which robbed Ellen of absolute triumph. One tiny slip, back on day 80, when she allowed herself a brief sleep in the Doldrums – not the hardest sailing by far, but as demanding in terms of crucial concentration as any – after a Herculanean struggle climbing the mast to mend the wind instruments, an endless night time battle worthy of a book or film in itself, and she had allowed Desjoyeaux, 'Mich' as she refers to him, to get the directional jump-start into the trade winds which he needed. After that it was always going to be hard for her to catch up. The astounding thing is that she almost made it.

Had it not been for her crashing into a floating container – one of many thousands dumped annually at sea – her daggerboard would not have been ruined. Even then, she effected repairs and motored on; it was only a couple of days ago, when her forestay unexpectedly went, that she knew the race was over; she could not pile the pressure on the mast without the risk of bringing it down.

Nevertheless, she knows, as she cruises in some time this evening, hoping furiously to catch the tide-barrier in time and enter Les Sables during the evening, rather than having to wait until the next morning, that what she has achieved is beyond any expectations. Beyond those of her parents, who hardly know what to make of their driven offspring; this is not a sailing family. Beyond the expectations of her homeland, which had forgotten how glorious its sailing tradition was and how one story could capture the imagination.

It has done so, quite simply, thanks to Ellen. She shared it with people, by phone links and email, and it was this vulnerable human element to the tale which held.

TASK

Investigate

The journalist writing this article obviously admires Ellen MacArthur, and his piece attempts to convince his readers of her qualities and achievements, although these are often implied, not stated directly.

Select **three qualities** in Ellen that the writer admires. List each in a table like the one below, and then select evidence from the text to illustrate the conclusion you have drawn. One has been completed for you.

Quality or achievement	Evidence
Determination	'Even then, she effected repairs'

TASK

Writing to inform

Your task is to write a short informative piece (for an encyclopaedia or a website entry) on Ellen MacArthur using the information from the two sources you have studied – her log entries and the newspaper article.

- ❏ This is a **timed** task.
- ❏ Spend **15 minutes making brief notes** of the **content** of the piece.
- ❏ Spend **10 minutes planning** the piece. You should write no more than three paragraphs. Cluster related information about Ellen MacArthur into each paragraph. Draft the topic sentence for each. Remember to plan how you will end the piece.
- ❏ **Write** for no more than **20 minutes**, including time to read back through and make necessary alterations.

Masterclass

- ◆ Use link words and phrases to join your ideas up within and across paragraphs. You might use a *pronoun* to avoid repeating a word or phrase e.g. '*This* was followed by…'. Try using *adverbials* to start sentences (but use them sparingly, and tellingly) e.g. '*Although she doesn't come from a sailing family*, Ellen…'
- ◆ Mainly use the present tense e.g. 'Ellen MacArthur is…'
- ◆ Think carefully about how you will end the piece. Perhaps try to draft your final sentence in advance and then write towards it.

Testing times

Enduring failure

> Men wanted for hazardous journey. Small wages. Bitter cold. Long months of complete darkness. Constant danger. Safe return doubtful. Honour and recognition in case of success. (Ernest Shackleton)

TASK

1. You have two minutes to speed read the following short information text. Remember: **skim** the passage by letting your eye run down the centre of the page, focusing in on key words and phrases to get the gist of the content.
2. Now, with a partner, see how much of the passage you can remember. What are the important details?
3. Re-read the passage. Pick out and copy the topic sentences for each paragraph. What do you notice about them?

In 1914, Sir Ernest Shackleton set out from England on a daring expedition. His goal: the first crossing of the Antarctic continent. This was not Shackleton's first journey to Antarctica. Like a handful of other explorers at the beginning of the 20th century, Shackleton had been determined to venture to the mysterious continent at the bottom of the earth. And although these early expeditions were intent on scientific advancement, the grand prize was the South Pole – unclaimed territory, where no human had ever stood.

Shackleton first headed south in 1901, accompanying Robert F. Scott on an unsuccessful bid for the Pole. Six years later Shackleton set out again, leading his own expedition south and coming within approximately 100 miles of his goal, further south than anyone had gone before. Here, taking stock of his party's failing supplies and health, Shackleton made the heartbreaking decision to turn back. In 1911, the race was finally won by Roald Amundsen of Norway.

In 1914, with the prize of the Pole having been claimed, Shackleton embarked on a new challenge – to cross the entire continent on foot, from the Weddell to the Ross Sea. Leaving the island of South Georgia in December, his ship Endurance battled her way through pack ice toward the continent. But while deep in the pack-ice of the Weddell Sea, the ship was trapped and slowly crushed by the ice. Shackleton and his men became castaways in one of the most hostile environments on earth. The expedition was a failure – yet the unimaginable saga of survival that followed ensured that it was for this, the failed Endurance expedition, that Shackleton is ultimately most remembered.

English Works

Eye-witness account

Now read this extract from Shackleton's own account of the journey on Endurance. He describes how the ship started to break up when trapped in pack ice:

The pressure was increasing steadily, and the passing hours brought no relief or respite for the ship. The attack of the ice reached its climax at 4pm. The ship was hove stern up by the pressure, and the driving floe, moving laterally across the stern, split the rudder and tore out the rudder-post and stern-post. Then, while we watched, the ice loosened and the *Endurance* sank a little. The decks were breaking upwards and the water was pouring in below. Again, the pressure began, and at 5pm I ordered all hands onto the ice. The twisting, grinding floes were working their will at last on the ship. It was a sickening sensation to feel the decks breaking up under one's feet, the great beams bending and then snapping with a noise like heavy gun-fire. The water was overmastering the pumps, and to avoid an explosion when it reached the boilers I had to give orders for the fires to be drawn and the steam let down.

The plans for abandoning the ship in the case of emergency had been made well in advance, and the men and dogs descended to the floe and made their way to the comparative safety of an unbroken portion of the floe without a hitch. Just before leaving, I looked down the engine-room skylight as I stood on the quivering deck, and saw the engines dropping sideways as the stays and bed-plates gave way. I cannot describe the impression of relentless destruction that was forced upon me as I looked down and around. The floes, with the force of millions of tons of moving ice behind them, were simply annihilating the ship.

TASK

❶ Annotate a copy of the above text to show the following:
  ❑ *Verbs* and *verbs used as adjectives* to convey the destructive action of the ice
  ❑ *Short sentences* used to mark key events
  ❑ *Temporal connectives* to link the action into a chronological sequence

❷ Discuss how the writer makes the ice seem to be an enemy of the ship.

Masterclass

Helping the reader to 'see it how it was'

An effective recount, such as an eye-witness account, helps the reader to 'see' events and actions as they unfold. This means including lots of descriptive detail by modifying verbs and nouns. You can do this by:

- Adding an adjective or an adjectival phrase to a noun: e.g. 'sickening sensation'; 'liquid surface of the sea'
- Linking an adverb with a verb: e.g. 'dropping sideways'
- Using a prepositional phrase: e.g. 'snapping with a noise like heavy gun-fire'
- Using *temporal connectives* e.g. *first, then, again, after this, just then…*

TASK

Choose one of the following writing tasks. You should write a short, compressed piece of descriptive writing in a single paragraph, designed to recreate the scene and the events as they unfolded. You were there, and your job as a writer is to 'take the reader there'. Base your writing on either a real or imagined event. Write in the first person, from the point of view of someone who was present – either watching or even participating. Include telling descriptions of what happened 'inside your head' as well as the outside events.

1. An exciting moment or incident in a recent sporting event.
2. A meeting between two friends who haven't seen each other for a long time.
3. Geography link: a natural disaster – for example, flood, fire, earthquake.
4. History link: a key moment or event – possibly written from the point of view of a participant.
5. A key incident from a novel you have been reading: retell it as an eye-witness account from the point of view of a character.

Marketing heroism

THE ENDURANCE:
Shackleton's Legendary Antarctic Expedition

EXPEDITION

EXHIBITION

IMAX™ MOVIE

The Exhibition, on view from April 10 – October 11, 1999 at the American Museum of Natural History, documented one of the greatest tales of survival in expedition history: Sir Ernest Shackleton's 1914 voyage to the Antarctic. Just one day's sail from the continent, the ship *Endurance* became trapped in sea ice. Frozen fast for ten months, the ship was crushed and destroyed by ice pressure, and the crew was forced to abandon ship. After camping on the ice for five months, Shackleton made two open boat journeys, one of which – a treacherous 800-mile ocean crossing to South Georgia Island – is now considered one of the greatest boat journeys in history. Trekking across the mountains of South Georgia, Shackleton reached the island's remote whaling station, organized a rescue team, and saved all of the men he had left behind.

The spectacular new giant-screen film, *Shackleton's Antarctic Adventure*, will immerse Museum visitors in the fierce cold and the extreme weather conditions of one of the most inhospitable places on earth. This 40-minute film brings to life the extraordinary true story of Sir Ernest Shackleton's ill-fated expedition to traverse the Antarctic. Haunting photographs and 35mm film footage taken by expedition photographer Frank Hurley, combined with dramatic re-enactments and breathtaking, giant-screen contemporary footage, enfold audiences into one of the most awesome man-against-nature sagas ever told.

© 1999–2001 The American Museum of Natural History. All Rights Reserved.

TASK

1. Discuss the overall purpose of this text.

2. Look again at the two paragraphs. Use a copy of the chart below to list three differences between them.

	Paragraph One	Paragraph Two
Vocabulary: choice of words and phrases		
Sentences: the way sentences are constructed		
Text: the purpose of each paragraph		

English Works

TASK

 Discuss how the following text makes use of **a range of different text types** in order to achieve its purpose of selling you a set of videos.

SHACKLETON – Kenneth Branagh
A&E Video

"Adrift at the bottom of the world, one man refused to abandon hope."

Now available in DVD and VHS we are pleased to offer the Collector's Edition of **SHACKLETON**.

"Men wanted for hazardous journey. Small wages. Bitter cold. Long months of complete darkness. Constant danger. Safe return doubtful. Honour and recognition in case of success." – Ernest Shackleton

The 27 men who joined his 1914 expedition to cross Antarctica found that Ernest Shackleton was true to his word. But what they endured was worse than anyone could have imagined. And their survival transformed the mission's initial failure into the greatest triumph from the age of polar exploration.

Based on the detailed diaries and first-person accounts of expedition members, **SHACKLETON** brings their harrowing ordeal to life, from the frustration as ice closed around their ship to the death-defying, 800-mile journey in an open boat across the world's worst seas that made their rescue possible.

Written and directed by BAFTA winner Charles Sturridge (*Longitude*, *Brideshead Revisited*), **SHACKLETON** stars multiple academy award nominee Kenneth Branagh (*Henry V*, *Hamlet*) as the legendary explorer.

An all-star cast featuring Kevin McNally (*Entrapment*), Nicholas Rowe (*Lock, Stock and Two Smoking Barrels*, *Longitude*), Chris Larkin (*Angels and Insects*, *Tea with Mussolini*), and Phoebe Nicholls (*Fairy Tale: A True Story*, *Persuasion*).

The DVD Deluxe Collector's Edition includes 3-discs packed with over 4 hours of bonus material. Featuring:

- 50-minute Featurette: *The Making of Shackleton* Ernest Shackleton Episode of A&E's Award Winning Series BIOGRAPHY
- 2-hour Bonus Programme From the History Channel: *Antarctica: A Frozen History*
- Biography/Filmography of Kenneth Branagh
- Interactive Menus
- Scene Selection

Collector's Edition (DVD) – 200 minutes + Extras (3-Discs)
Collector's Edition (VHS) – 200 minutes total (4-Videos)
NOW IN STOCK!!! These videos will ship Next Business Day.

Masterclass

Writing to persuade the reader to buy

Effective persuasive writing quickly gains the attention of the reader and then attempts to influence (or manipulate) the reader's response towards a specific end.

Try:

- Starting with an eye-catching slogan or opening sentence
- Using direct quotation
- Including key information to make the product seem essential
- Including persuasive vocabulary, especially adjectives and adverbs
- Using wordplay to make the text lively and memorable
- Addressing the reader directly using the second person ('you')
- Experimenting with different font sizes and page layout (especially if you are able to use ICT for this task)

TASK

Select one of the following tasks.

Compose a short page of text that combines information, persuasive language and textual features in order to either:

1. Market a video version of the Shakespeare play you have been studying in Year 9;
2. Market a film or video version of a novel you have read or studied recently;
3. Advertise a local attraction for visitors to your area; or
4. Advertise a new website devoted to the exploits of Ellen MacArthur (using information from your work in the earlier part of this unit).

They came from the deep

Giant Squid washed up on a beach near Hobart

On Saturday 20 July, 2002, Tasmanian Museum zoologists were notified by Parks and Wildlife Staff of a Giant Squid on Seven Mile Beach.

The Squid had washed ashore earlier that morning and by the time it was collected had broken into two pieces, but was still remarkably fresh. This is the third time in recent times that a giant squid has washed ashore in Southern Tasmania. It is interesting that all have been found on or around the 20 of July. The first was in 1986, then again in 1992 and this animal.

Although always thought to live in deep oceans, the freshness of this specimen makes us think that it was alive in the coastal waters off Tasmania. We wonder if these squid which, like other squid, probably have a synchronised breeding season, are breeding in local waters.

The squid weighs about 250 kg and was found to be a recently mated female. We know this because small sperm packets were found imbedded just under the mantle. In this way the female squid stores the sperm to fertilise her eggs later. Her body also showed signs of a passionate embrace, there were sucker marks on her neck and a nip on her head from the male's beak.

Some samples have been taken to age the animal and also to assess the molecular variation between populations.

Tasmania is also the home of the world's smallest squid, Southern Pygmy Squid. These are 2 cm long. A fascinating fact about giant squid is that they grow from a few centimeters to 15 m in three or four years and the muscle structure to allow this growth is exactly the same shape and size of the Pygmy Squid.

TASK

This text mixes two key text types: **recount** (in the style of a newspaper account of an incident) and **report** (an account of 'the way things are').

1. On a copy of the text, use two highlighters to mark the sections which are a report and those which are a recount.
2. Use two different colour highlighter pens to mark examples on a copy of the above text of the use of active and passive voice. Select one example of each and explain why the writer chose to use this voice.

# TASK

Now read the following passage. It is taken from a scientific report about giant squid. But notice how the writer has made some attempts, despite the complex scientific language, to make the information accessible to the non-specialist reader. Discuss those features of the text which help the non-specialist. Which sections of this are more difficult to read and understand?

As you read the passage, make note of where you use the following reading strategies:

❑ Phonic knowledge and skill (the sounds that various letters and letter combinations make; segmenting words into parts and putting the whole word together bit by bit)
❑ Using your knowledge of other words (word associations and word families) in order to work out what a word or phrase might mean
❑ Using your knowledge of how words fit together in sentences to help you make sense of an unknown word
❑ Making an educated guess at the meaning of a word or phrase, based on your general knowledge, and on what you already know about giant squid
❑ Re-reading a sentence a few times in order to get the sense of it (this is particularly useful with complex sentences containing multiple layers of meaning)

Architeuthis, or the giant squid, is a cephalopod like an octopus or nautilus. They are even related to such common animals as snails.

The giant squid inhabits all the oceans of the world and has been linked to all the continents. Possessing a complex brain and the largest eye of any known animal we can only speculate as to how keen of perception this mysterious creature is.

The only specimens available for study have been dead. Most often these carcasses are in poor condition and in all likelihood were sick or injured prior to death giving us a less then perfect picture of how this creature lives.

Although squid beachings and capture by deep water fishing trawl are fairly common we have yet to study this animal in its natural habitat. This is due in large part to the depth at which the giant squid lives. They have adapted their bodies to live in neutral buoyancy by forfeiting the typical salt in their body fluids with the far lighter compound of ammonium chloride. This allows the squid to stay stable and quite comfortable at about two thousand feet below the ocean's surface.

Only in the past twenty years have we had the kind of deep dive technology required to venture so far into the open ocean. Most of the deep sea is still unexplored and our technological and financial limitations for explorative dives prevent sustained surveillance efforts. Perhaps in years to come as man's needs for deep-sea resources grows and submersible travel becomes common place more mysteries like those of Architeuthis will be revealed for study.

Source: © 2001 Tribe City Group, Inc., http://www.giantsquidcenter.com/

English Works

A fight with a giant squid

The final section of this unit leads up to **an extended writing task**, where you will be composing and constructing a piece of narrative writing. In a few moments you will be reading and talking in depth about a section from Jules Verne's famous novel *Twenty Thousand Leagues Under the Sea*. It was written in 1873. When it was published it was regarded as a 'science fiction' novel as it speculated about what would happen if a submarine could be invented that could travel by generating its own electric power from seawater, and that was capable of submerging to huge depths.

> **Key characters:**
>
> Captain Nemo – the commander of the submarine
>
> Ned Land – a Canadian seaman and professional harpooner
>
> The narrator – a French professor of natural history (biologist) and his servant, Conseil
>
> The Nautilus – the name of the submarine

You will need to read the sections that follow 'with a writer's eye'. Store up techniques and 'tricks of the trade' that the author employs in order to tell the story. Look out in particular for:

- how to move the narrative on
- how to convey the feelings of a character through what they say
- how to bring the reader 'into' the story
- how to convey action
- how to hint at things that remain just 'under the surface' of the text, conveying more than is actually stated in words, so that the reader has to do some working out for themselves

And enjoy the narrative as it unfolds!

Before my eyes was a horrible monster worthy to figure in the legends of the marvellous. It was an immense cuttlefish, being eight yards long. It swam crossways in the direction of the Nautilus with great speed, watching us with its enormous staring green eyes. Its eight arms, or rather feet, fixed to its head, that have given the name of cephalopod to these animals, were twice as long as its body, and were twisted like the furies' hair. One could see the 250 air-holes on the inner side of the tentacles. The monster's mouth, a horned beak like a parrot's, opened and shut vertically. Its tongue, a horned substance, furnished with several rows of pointed teeth, came out quivering from this veritable pair of shears. What a freak of nature, a bird's beak on a mollusc! Its spindle-like body formed a fleshy mass that might weigh 4,000 to 5,000 lb.; the varying colour changing with great rapidity, according to the irritation of the animal, passed successively from livid grey to reddish brown. What irritated this mollusc? No doubt the presence of the Nautilus, more formidable than itself, and on which its suckers or its jaws had no hold. Yet, what monsters these poulps are! what vitality the Creator has given them! what vigour in their movements! and they possess three hearts! Chance had brought us in presence of this cuttlefish, and I did not wish to lose the opportunity of carefully studying this specimen of cephalopods. I overcame the horror that inspired me, and, taking a pencil, began to draw it.

TASK

❶ Investigate the text to find out:
- ❏ exactly what the giant squid looked like. If you have an artistic streak, you could do what the narrator did and draw the creature!
- ❏ how the narrator conveys the impression that the squid is a monster. Look especially at the adjectives and images he uses to describe it

❷ What does the narrator think and feel about the huge squid? Look for evidence that he is both horrified and fascinated.

❸ From this passage, what do we learn about the narrator?

Testing times

Now: read on

> By this time other poulps appeared at the port light. I counted seven. They formed a procession after the Nautilus, and I heard their beaks gnashing against the iron hull. I continued my work. These monsters kept in the water with such precision that they seemed immovable. Suddenly the Nautilus stopped. A shock made it tremble in every plate.
>
> A minute passed. Captain Nemo, followed by his lieutenant, entered the drawing-room. I had not seen him for some time. He seemed dull. Without noticing or speaking to us, he went to the panel, looked at the poulps, and said something to his lieutenant. The latter went out. Soon the panels were shut. The ceiling was lighted. I went towards the Captain.
>
> "A curious collection of poulps?" I said.
> "Yes, indeed, Mr. Naturalist," he replied; "and we are going to fight them, man to beast."
> I looked at him. I thought I had not heard aright.
> "Man to beast?" I repeated.
> "Yes, sir. The screw is stopped. I think that the horny jaws of one of the cuttlefish are entangled in the blades. That is what prevents our moving."
> "What are you going to do?"
> "Rise to the surface, and slaughter this vermin."
> "A difficult enterprise."
> "Yes, indeed. The electric bullets are powerless against the soft flesh, where they do not find resistance enough to go off. But we shall attack them with the hatchet."
> "And the harpoon, sir," said the Canadian, "if you do not refuse my help."
> "I will accept it, Master Land."
> "We will follow you," I said, and, following Captain Nemo, we went towards the central staircase.

TASK

1. Investigate this section in order to work out **how the writer**:
   - ❏ Moves the action on by using temporal connectives and short sentences
   - ❏ Punctuates and sets out direct speech
   - ❏ Conveys a character's feelings and inner thoughts through what he or she says
   - ❏ Conveys more to the reader than is actually stated

2. From what Captain Nemo says and does, what evidence is there from this extract that this isn't his first encounter with a giant squid?

English Works

Now: read on

There, about ten men with boarding-hatchets were ready for the attack. Conseil and I took two hatchets; Ned Land seized a harpoon. The Nautilus had then risen to the surface. One of the sailors, posted on the top ladderstep, unscrewed the bolts of the panels. But hardly were the screws loosed, when the panel rose with great violence, evidently drawn by the suckers of a poulp's arm. Immediately one of these arms slid like a serpent down the opening and twenty others were above. With one blow of the axe, Captain Nemo cut this formidable tentacle, that slid wriggling down the ladder. Just as we were pressing one on the other to reach the platform, two other arms, lashing the air, came down on the seaman placed before Captain Nemo, and lifted him up with irresistible power. Captain Nemo uttered a cry, and rushed out. We hurried after him.

What a scene! The unhappy man, seized by the tentacle and fixed to the suckers, was balanced in the air at the caprice of this enormous trunk. He rattled in his throat, he was stifled, he cried, 'Help! help!' That heart-rending cry! I shall hear it all my life. The unfortunate man was lost. Who could rescue him from that powerful pressure? However, Captain Nemo had rushed to the poulp, and with one blow of the axe had cut through one arm. His lieutenant struggled furiously against other monsters that crept on the flanks of the Nautilus. The crew fought with their axes. The Canadian, Conseil, and I buried our weapons in the fleshy masses; a strong smell of musk penetrated the atmosphere. It was horrible!

For one instant, I thought the unhappy man, entangled with the poulp, would be torn from its powerful suction. Seven of the eight arms had been cut off. One only wriggled in the air, brandishing the victim like a feather. But just as Captain Nemo and his lieutenant threw themselves on it, the animal ejected a stream of black liquid. We were blinded with it. When the cloud dispersed, the cuttlefish had disappeared, and my unfortunate countryman with it. Ten or twelve poulps now invaded the platform and sides of the Nautilus. We rolled pell-mell into the midst of this nest of serpents, that wriggled on the platform in the waves of blood and ink. It seemed as though these slimy tentacles sprang up like the hydra's heads. Ned Land's harpoon, at each stroke, was plunged into the staring eyes of the cuttlefish. But my bold companion was suddenly overturned by the tentacles of a monster he had not been able to avoid.

Ah! how my heart beat with emotion and horror! The formidable beak of a cuttlefish was open over Ned Land. The unhappy man would be cut in two. I rushed to his succour. But Captain Nemo was before me; his axe disappeared between the two enormous jaws, and, miraculously saved, the Canadian, rising, plunged his harpoon deep into the triple heart of the poulp.

'I owed myself this revenge!' said the Captain to the Canadian.

Ned bowed without replying. The combat had lasted a quarter of an hour. The monsters, vanquished and mutilated, left us at last, and disappeared under the waves. Captain Nemo, covered with blood, nearly exhausted, gazed upon the sea that had swallowed up one of his companions, and great tears gathered in his eyes.

Testing times

TASK

❶ How are different types of sentences **combined** to show the detail of what happened and also keep the action moving on? Look for **complex** sentences beginning with **adverbials** such as 'for one instant', and extra details in subordinate clauses such as 'that slid wriggling down the ladder.' How are these combined with short, simple sentences?

❷ How does the author **end** this episode? Look especially at the final two sentences. Can you see a **pattern** in these sentences?

TASK

Use what you have learned about writing an **action narrative** to write **an extended episode** in a story where there is an emphasis on keeping up the *pace* of the narrative.

The task does not require you to compose a complete story – rather to select a key episode from a story and to compose it carefully, using and experimenting with what you have learned from this part of the unit.

- *Select* an episode – this could be from a story you have already written. Now's your chance to rework and improve it. Or go to a well-known story and select an event to rework, perhaps writing from the point of view of one or more characters. Or invent a completely new idea.
- *Brainstorm and map out* your idea first. Keep it simple: a couple of characters, a key event – perhaps a confrontation, or an accident, or a moment of fear. It could be as simple as taking your character into a room, or a strange place, and making something happen there, e.g. two teenagers go into a park and one of them gets attacked by a savage dog.
- *Remember* – you don't need to write all the introductory part. Just start right at the point where the action begins.
- *Draft your piece,* aiming as you write to incorporate techniques and tricks of the trade from your reading of the Jules Verne piece. Think *cinematically.* How would it look? What key action should I zoom in on?
- *Review and revise as you go.* Read aloud. Try the next sentence on for size before you write it. Go back and improve by adding detail, removing bits that don't contribute, intensify the language. Vary your sentences for effect.
- *Try your writing out on someone else.* Work with a partner and stop periodically to help each other by reading aloud and offering helpful comments.

English Works

Masterclass

Writing an action narrative

- Use dialogue sparingly, to precede the action, or to conclude it with a conversation. Aim to convey more than is stated in the actual words – for example, how a character is feeling
- Use a combination of long, complex and short simple sentences for effect
- Use action verbs and adverbs to convey *exactly* how something happens
- Move the narrative on by using *temporal connectives* – such as 'just then', 'at that moment', 'all at once', 'as soon as'
- Experiment with 'multiple narrative' where you describe events from two or more different perspectives
- Find a satisfying way of rounding off the episode. Try to use a concluding line of dialogue, or a sentence which uses the technique adopted by Jules Verne, where the *effect* of the action on a character is described. Stories are often about how a character has changed – so show this change by the end of your episode

Answers to *What, where, when and why*

1. Extract from newspaper article about Ellen MacArthur, round-the-world yachtswoman, from the *Observer*, February 2001.
2. Extract from newspaper report of finding of giant squid. From the *Independent*, August 2002.
3. Extract from advertisement for special offer of a boxed set of DVDs and videos.
4. Extract from Jules Verne's fictional account of an attack by a giant squid from *Twenty Thousand Leagues Under the Sea* (1873).
5. Extract from Ellen MacArthur's email log of her participation in a round-the-world race (2001).
6. Scientific report (from a website specialising in information about giant squid).

English Works

UNIT 4 Taking control

KEY OBJECTIVES

In this unit you will learn about the following key objectives:

High frequency words – how to remember tricky words which regularly crop up in your writing

Evaluate own spelling – ways of analysing your own spelling problems so that you can devise efficient strategies to check and correct your work

During the course of this unit, the emphasis will be on you to become self-sufficient as a speller. Quite simply, this means that you will learn how to tackle every key word that you encounter in school, plus a few more.

You will have the opportunity to compile your own Concise Personal Spellchecker, so that you can have a portable 'ready-reckoner' to guide your spelling at all times. Of course, there will be moments when you have to 'think on your feet' as a speller, especially in tests and exams, so there are some sections of this unit which have been designed to help you do just that.

Learning to spell should not be simply a series of dull routines. You will find a range of game-based activities which nearly always involve you working with other people to support each other's development as spellers. However, the emphasis is on you being able to research key words, invent strategies which work for you and set targets for yourself, so that your learning becomes ever-more independent, enjoyable and fulfilling.

English Works

Spotting the problems

As writers, we all are prone to making spelling mistakes. This could be because the process of writing, what to say and how to phrase the words, takes our attention away from spelling. So, to be accurate as well as fluent writers, we need some strategies to help us.

Spelling mistakes tend to occur in two basic ways.

1. The first type of spelling mistake is the sort that is easy to put right. As soon as we cast our eyes over the page, they become glaringly obvious. If you are using a keyboard, misspellings such as 'hte' instead of 'the' are quite common and easily rectified, especially if you are using a spellchecker. This spelling error is sometimes called a 'typo' because it is associated with typing and keyboards. The straightforward approach to correcting this first type of spelling mistake is proofreading, either as you write or when you have finished a draft.

2. The second type of spelling mistake is more problematic because it indicates that there is a specific spelling rule or convention which you haven't yet grasped. An example of this would be: 'rythm' for 'rhythm'. Clearly, in this example, the writer has not just made a 'careless' error. This writer is not aware of: the 'rh' rule – many words which begin with the /r/ sound and are followed by a vowel sound often have an 'h' following the 'r'. For instance, 'rhino', 'rhyme' and 'rhapsody'.

TASK

1. Working in pairs, consult a dictionary. Look for words beginning with 'rh' and find ten examples. What is the word origin of your examples? The clue to spelling the 'rh' words is their word origin. Most of them come from ancient Greek and they have kept their old Greek spelling pattern of 'rh'.

2. Now complete a copy of the spelling audit below, for the work of two pupils. Stay in your pairs and read the two examples overleaf. The task is for you to proofread their writing, spot the simple errors (Type one), the problems (Type two) and suggest correction strategies.

Word	Spelling Error Type one	Correction strategy…	Spelling Error Type two	Correction strategy…
Audit conclusions:				

English Works

Taking control

These Year 9 pupils have been asked to write a paragraph explaining their views on young people and politics to an audience of local councillors.

Pupil A

> The resons why young peple don't intrested in poiltics is becorse politicuns don't ever speak to us. When we want to tell them about ower veiws like haveing a youth club, they don't listen and so we get turned off politics. I like talking with my mates about things that are happening so why don't politicuns come and ask us what we think?

Pupil B

> Youn people are genrally not interested in politics because it seems to be about older people and issues which are not really relevant to us. But I think politics should be about things that really matter to us. We should be allowed to talk about drugs and relationships and whether we want a by-pass building, even though we're not voting yet. How can we get excited about voting if no-one lets us talk about these things before we're eighteen?

TASK

1. After completing the audit exercise, write a short paragraph summarising your correction strategy recommendations for both pupils.

2. Discuss your findings by comparing your suggestions with others in your class.
   To make effective improvements yourself, you need to be able to analyse the pattern of your own spelling errors. The next exercise is designed to help you do that.

3. Skim read through examples of your own writing. This could be in your English work or any other subject-based writing which you have available. In fact, if you have personal writing to hand, you could include this as well. As you read, use a Concise Personal Spellchecker to help you record, and reflect on, your own error patterns. This should be a table listing your spelling errors, specific examples and your correction strategies.

English Works

Derivations: investigating word histories

1. Working with a partner, explain to each other two personal spelling strategies which you have recorded in your Concise Personal Spellchecker. Share these ideas with the rest of the group and make a display of your findings.
2. Being able to spell accurately is a skill for life. To become a really efficient and accurate speller, you need to be able to tackle difficult words in all subject areas, not just English.
3. Working in pairs, choose eight more words from the key word banks and mount your own investigation. Report your findings to the group.

Spelling patterns often occur because words have similar histories. They may have been used in many languages before they came into English.

Look at these examples of investigations into a word's history:

Word	Meaning	Common Misspelling	Derivation	Spelling Strategy
1. Negative	A minus number	Negitive	From the Latin 'negaratum' meaning to deny	A linked modern word is 'negate' – to deny something. The 'ate' split digraph means the word 'negative' must have an 'a' not an 'i'.
2. Laboratory	Place where experiments	Laborotory	From the Latin word for 'work': 'labor'	This word can be split in half – 'labor' from the Latin for 'work' and 'atory' meaning a room – labor-atory (as in 'conserv-atory').

English Works

Many words have common spelling patterns. Look at these examples from the subject spelling lists:

Maths Key Words	Common Links and Spelling Patterns	Science Key Words
1. circumference	Notice the common prefix to these words 'circ' which derives from the Latin word 'circus' meaning a ring.	1. circulate
2. fraction	Only the single vowel sound is different. However, they have different roots. 'Fract' comes from the Latin word 'fractum' meaning to break whereas 'frict' the prefix of 'friction' comes from the Latin word 'frictum' meaning to rub.	2. friction

❶ Now, examine the key word banks from Science and Maths and complete your own investigations into common spelling patterns and links between the words from each subject area. Find ten pairs of words which are linked in some way e.g. prefixes, suffixes or common letter strings. You will need a dictionary on hand to help your investigation. Three examples are given below.

Maths Key Words	Common Links and Spelling Patterns	Science Key Words
reflect	Focus on prefixes e.g. 're'	respire
addition	Focus on suffixes e.g. 'tion'	circulation
questionnaire	Focus on double letters e.g. 'nn'/'dd'	mammal

❷ Report back your findings to the whole group.
❸ Write any specific examples which you feel you need to remember in your Concise Personal Spellchecker. Self-test yourself on five words by using the Look/Write/Cover/Say/Check method.

Take your spelling for a walk

❶ Check your Concise Personal Spellchecker and find one particularly tricky word, which you have recently learnt. Add this word to a class list. There should be about twenty-five words in total. Then, working with a partner, jot down as many words as you can remember without looking at the list. Remember, they should all be correctly spelt! Finally, check which pair has remembered the most words correctly.

Now that you have completed your investigation of Maths and Science key words, you need to go a step further and review the remaining key words from other subject areas. You are going to 'take your spelling for a walk' by working together to analyse your awareness of these other key words. In the boxes below, there are extracts from the subject specific word banks.

❷ Scan the first subject box and find a word which you have difficulty spelling. Text mark a copy of it and, in the space next to it, jot down a personal strategy to help you remember it. Then, move on to the second subject box and repeat the process. When you have twelve words, spend a couple of minutes visualising each of the words, before your partner tests you on them. An example is given below.

Geography

Landscape
Infrastructure
International
Latitude
Pollution

Strategy 1 for: 'Infrastructure'
Made up of two sections – 'infra' from the Latin meaning 'below' and 'structure,' means how something is put together from the Latin 'structum' to build. Remember the two parts, the 'a' in 'infra' and the 'u' at the end.

Strategy 2 for: 'Dynasty'
The phoneme /i/ is spelt with a 'y'. To remember this I will pronounce the word as if it has a capital 'I', D-I-n-a-s-t-y.

History

Disease
Dynasty
Priest
Rebellion
Bias
Reign

English Works

Taking control

TASK continued

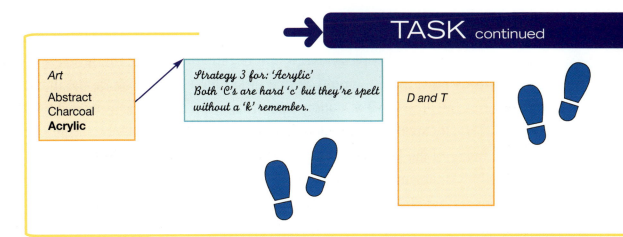

Art
Abstract
Charcoal
Acrylic

Strategy 3 for: 'Acrylic'
Both 'C's are hard 'c' but they're spelt without a 'k' remember.

D and T

TASK

❶ Your task now is to examine all of the subject spelling lists and find one word from each area to learn.

❷ The trick is to remember these key spellings. Using a copy of the 'Take your spelling for a walk' Personal Analysis Sheet below, complete the entries for your words.

❸ When you have done this, extend the list by collecting any difficult words you come across in the next twenty-four hours. Keep your sheet and a pencil handy and just note them down. They could be on advertising hoardings, buses or shop fronts. You might find them in newspapers, magazines or even on the television. Wherever they are, blitz them for a day and see what kind of lexicon, or word bank, emerges.

'Take your spelling for a walk' Personal Analysis Sheet		
Location	Spelling Issue	Strategy
1. Geography spelling bank	Infrastructure	1. Remember the two parts
2. The *Guardian* newspaper	Correspondent	2. Syllabification 'co-rres-pon-dent' + roll the 'r' when I say = double 'r'
3. Shakespeare	Soliloquy	3. It's got 'lilo' in the middle
4.		
5.		
6.		

English Works   71

Shakespearian spelling

As Shakespeare wrote his plays during the Elizabethan era, many of the spellings seem unusual to us now. In fact, writers at that time didn't have to abide by all our rules and conventions because there was no generally accepted spelling system. However, being able to correctly spell Shakespearian terms is important to us now. This section draws together many of the key terms from the various plays in Year 9 so that you can consider your spelling strategies.

The words have been divided into three categories: Characters' names, Place names and Theatrical terms.

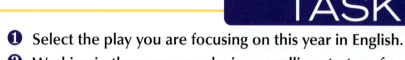

1. Select the play you are focusing on this year in English.
2. Working in three groups, devise a spelling strategy for the words listed below. You will find it more efficient to allocate a small number of words to pairs of people within your group.

Characters' names in Shakespeare's plays can be very tricky. They often have unusual letter patterns and, indeed, they may even be foreign names. Decide on a spelling strategy for each of the characters in your chosen play. (N.B. Not all of the characters are represented here but these are the names which seem to require some attention.)

Henry V
Gloster
Salisbury
Westmoreland
Warwick
Scroop
Erpingham
Fluellen
Falstaff
Dauphin
Rambures
Grandpree

Twelfth Night
Antonio   Malvolio
Valentine   Fabian
Ague-cheek   Sebastian
Viola

Macbeth
Donalbain   Siward
Banquo   Seyton
Macduff   Hecate
Fleance   Malcolm

English Works

Taking control

Henry V
Eastcheap
Harfleur
Rouen
Picardy
Agincourt

TASK

Place names in Shakespearian plays are often quite exotic. So, they need special strategies to help you to learn them. Decide on a spelling strategy for each of the following place names for your chosen play.

Twelfth Night
Illyria

Macbeth
Heath
Forres
Dunsinane
Inverness

Concise Personal Spellchecker – Shakespearian Spelling		
Place Name	**Spelling Issue**	**Strategy**
1. Illyria	The double 'l' in the name and the /i/ sound is a 'y'	1. The first three letters are like a set of cricket stumps and the rest of the word is the same as Syria

Soliloquy
Playwright
Characters
Dialogue
Tragedy
Theatre

TASK

Theatrical terms are common to many eras but they are relevant to your study of Shakespeare. Find strategies for learning the terms you add to this list.

Comedy
Costume
Dramatic irony
Director
Farce
Lighting
Rehearsal

Concise Personal Spellchecker – Shakespearian Spelling		
Theatrical Term	**Spelling Issue**	**Strategy**
1. Playwright	The last syllable is tricky – 'wright' has a silent 'w'. It comes from the old English word for work 'wryhta' as in shipwright	1. Try 'say – spell' and pronounce it 'play-W-right'.

English Works

The parallel process

Part of the problem with spelling is that we have to try to spell words correctly at the same time as we are thinking of the words and sentences we need to create meaning. This parallel process is tricky because it means that we are often thinking about two things at once. Of course, proofreading helps us to correct any of these mistakes but it is quicker and more efficient to be able to spell correctly as we write. To be able to do this, we need to practise.

You are going to explore the writing process now to discover what happens to you as you write and spell simultaneously. The example on this page gives you a model of how that might work. The writing in the table is from a Year 9 imaginative task for an audience of secondary pupils and/or adults entitled: 'The School of the Future.'

The Parallel Process – Simultaneous Spelling and Writing		
Spelling	**Writing**	**Commentary**
1. whirred	The particle beam transporter whirred as it began the process of school deliveries. The dial was set to St Aiden's and deliveries began at 7.45am. Hurriedly, I gulped down my toast and tea. Missing the transporter meant a walk to school. Strange to think that in my parent's day I might have to go by bus.	1. 'whirred' always confuses me but I think I've got it because it's got the 'wh' of 'when' and the double letters of 'stirred'
2. particle		2. 'particle' …

TASK

Working in pairs, write another paragraph to the story. As you write, keep a note of the words you come across which require you to consciously think about their spelling. After the paragraph is completed, discuss with each other how you came to spell the words and jot down your conclusions.

High frequency words

Many misspellings turn up time and time again. These are known as 'high frequency words' and, to be an efficient and accurate speller, you need to know how to spell these words almost automatically.

The first category of high frequency words you will consider deals with 'homophones' (from 'homo' meaning 'the same' and 'phone' meaning 'sound'). Homophones are those confusing words which have the same sound but different spellings and meanings. For instance, 'there', 'their', 'they're' are homophones which pupils often confuse. However, it is perfectly possible to apply spelling strategies to homophones to help you to be clear about their spellings and their meanings.

Look at the example in the table.

High Frequency Words	
Homophones	Strategy
1. Practise/practice	1. These homophones are often confused because they are grammatically different as well as being spelt differently. A good way to remember the difference is to remember that 'p-r-a-c-t-i-c-e' is the noun and it has the noun 'ice' in the word. Therefore the word 'p-r-a-c-t-i-s-e' is always used when the sentence calls for a verb.

Using the homophone list below and working in groups of four, divide the homophones up between you and devise strategies to learn the different spellings and when to use them. A light-hearted but effective way to learn spellings is to use rhymes or nonsense lines. For instance, 'the **witch** with an **itch** dropped her **stitch**'. All of the rhyming 'itch' words end with the same letter patterns.

Homophone List			
for/four	would/wood	through/threw	allowed/aloud
there/they're/their	our/hour	way/weigh	sites/sights
your/you're	what/watt	hear/here	sauce/source
one/won	which/witch	know/no	night/knight
where/wear	heard/herd	course/coarse	days/daze
saw/sore/soar	morning/mourning	braking/breaking	side/sighed
to/two/too			

Another source of confusion in spelling is a category of words known as 'heteronyms' (from 'hetero' meaning 'different' and 'nym' meaning 'name'). These are words which are spelt the same but which have different pronunciations and meanings. For instance, the word 'live' can be pronounced with a short vowel – 'live' meaning to exist – or with a long vowel – 'live' meaning 'happening now' as in a 'live' rock concert.

Working in pairs, use the heteronym list below to devise strategies for learning the different meanings and pronunciations. Copy them into a grid like you did for the homophones. You will need a dictionary to help you with this task. Below the list is an example of what your grid might look like.

Heteronym List
buffet, sewer, lead, read, tear, wind, wound, bow, entrance, row, sow, live

High Frequency Words	
Heteronym	Strategy – meaning and pronunciation
1. tear	1. This word could be 'tear' as in 'tear a cloth' or 'tear' as in 'crying'. Pronunciation and meaning could be remembered by rhyming it with 'wear' which is a verb. If it rhymes with 'wear' then it is the verb.

There is another category of words which cause confusion simply because they are similar:

Common Word Confusions			
advice/advise	choose/chose	affect/effect	quiet/quite

❶ Add strategies to your list to help you remember these confusing words.
❷ Still working in pairs, swap exercise books and look for any examples of high frequency spelling errors. Mark them in different coloured pen and pass them back. You now need to jot down these errors on your high frequency spellings page and learn them.

English Works

Taking control

Mrs T's spelling game

It's time to put all of your spelling knowledge to the test. However, you are not going to have a formal test. This test takes the form of a game; Mrs T's Spelling Game. Before you begin, you might want to quickly browse through your Concise Personal Spellchecker to remind yourself of those tricky words once again.

❶ Arrange your classroom so that there are two rows of pupils facing each other with the blackboard (or whiteboard) at one end (as in the photograph overleaf).

Rules of Mrs T's Spelling Game

1. This is a competition between two teams. The first team to correctly spell each word, wins the round.
2. The winner is the group in the lead at the end of the session.
3. Each person on each team is allocated a letter or letters.
4. The teacher, or leader, will read out a word and the appropriate person (letter) on each team will need to run to the board in the correct letter order to write it.
5. Only one person on each team is allowed out of their seats at any given time.
6. The team with the correct spelling, sitting down first, wins the round.
7. Talking is essential between team members.
8. Each team is allocated one half of the board as 'theirs' for writing the spellings.

❷ Now, listen carefully for the spelling word, support each other by suggesting which letter should be next and work together for success. The spellers who are the best collaborators will be the winners.

English Works

TASK

 Working with a partner, discuss which words you had trouble spelling under pressure. Add these to your Concise Personal Spellchecker because you will need a more efficient strategy to learn them.

English Works

Bringing it all together

Spelling is never easy but it is possible to make learning more fun by using the strategies in this unit and those you may have completed in Years 7 and 8. However, you are the only one who can really make it work.

TASK

1. Working as a whole class, identify all of the different spelling strategies you have used. Go back as far as primary school if you can remember.

2. Working with a partner, prepare a short talk of about two minutes which describes your own spelling style. How do you best learn spellings? Are you a visual speller or do you prefer a range of other spelling strategies?

3. Look back over the work you have done in this unit, make a list, then orally rehearse what you are going to say in pairs, see below for an example.

> Looking back over the words which I find difficult and the strategies I have used to overcome the problem, I think I have a bias towards visualising. I am lucky because I seem to be able to picture a word and its shape and remember it fairly quickly. An example of this is the word 'submarine'. I can see the periscope coming up in the middle of the word and it's there in my mind's eye.
>
> Sometimes, I need to use other strategies, though, and my particular favourite is 'say-spell'. It sounds ridiculous at times but saying 'b-e-a-u-t-i-f-u-l' sounding out each letter is a 'sure fire' way of getting the spelling right. It just seems to work for me.
>
> There are still some words which trouble me. Even though I know that 'relevant' has two 'e's then an 'a' I still want to put the 'a' in the middle. So, this is one of my target spellings over the next few weeks. I have thirty target words which are in my Concise Personal Spellchecker and my confidence is increasing all the time.

Henry V	*Twelfth Night*		*Macbeth*	
Gloster	Antonio	Malvolio	Donalbain	Siward
Salisbury	Valentine	Fabian	Banquo	Seyton
Westmoreland	Ague-cheek	Sebastian	Macduff	Hecate
Warwick	Viola		Fleance	Malcolm
Scroop				
Erpingham				
Fluellen				
Falstaff				
Dauphin				
Rambures				
Grandpree				

Rules of Mrs T's Spelling Game

1. This is a competition between two teams. The first team to correctly spell each word, wins the round.
2. The winner is the group in the lead at the end of the session.
3. Each person on each team is allocated a letter or letters.
4. The teacher, or leader, will read out a word and the appropriate person (letter) on each team will need to run to the board in the correct letter order to write it
5. Only one person on each team is allowed out of their seats at any given time.
6. The team with the correct spelling, sitting down first, wins the round.
7. Talking is essential between team members.
8. Each team is allocated one half of the board as 'theirs' for writing the spellings.

Strategy 1 for: 'Infrastructure'
Made up of two sections – 'infra' from the Latin meaning 'below' and 'structure' means how something is put together from the Latin 'structum' to build. Remember the two parts, the 'a' in 'infra' and the 'u' at the end.

Geography
Landscape
Infrastructure
International
Latitude
Pollution

TASK

❶ Deliver your talk to the class.
❷ Listen to other people's talks and notice where they differ from you as a speller. Which strategies seem to be the most popular in the group?

English Works

UNIT 5 Exploring scenes from Shakespeare

KEY OBJECTIVES

In this unit you will learn about the following key objectives:

Layers of meaning – looking closely at the different meanings and associations of words

Sustained Standard English – using formal language throughout a piece of writing

Formal essay – writing fluently, formally and accurately about Shakespeare, in timed conditions

Balanced analysis – writing analytically, bearing in mind a range of evidence and opinions

Considered viewpoint – discussing the range of evidence before deciding on your own views

Compare interpretations – discussing different points of view about an aspect of the play

In your end of key stage tests, you will have to answer two questions in the Shakespeare paper. The first is a short writing task, where the focus is on concise and precise writing in a particular style. The second question is a reading response, where you need to demonstrate your understanding of the Shakespeare text you have read in class. It is assumed you have already studied a Shakespeare play in detail. The purpose of this unit is to help you re-visit the specific skills you need to tackle the reading response successfully.

The objectives listed above are all vital if you are going to achieve your best on section B of the Shakespeare paper. 'Layers of meaning' is a word level objective that focuses on the effect of vocabulary choices. You already know that many words have connotations or associations. Shakespeare's careful choice of words indicates how he feels about characters, what they are saying or how they are behaving. The implied meanings of words or their associations can influence the way the audience views the characters and action.

English Works

For example, all these nouns are to do with leadership and power: tyrant, leader, despot, king, dictator, monarch and ruler. Most of us would agree that tyrant, despot, or dictator all have negative connotations, whereas the words leader, ruler, monarch and king are more neutral.

The 'Sustained Standard English' and 'Formal essay' objectives are closely linked. In both your Year 9 test and in your forthcoming GCSE course, you will be required to write formal essays, often in timed conditions and in a style appropriate to your reader and purpose. You will need to write confidently in Standard English and structure your essays so the reader finds it easy to follow your line of thought.

'Balanced analysis', 'Considered viewpoint' and 'Compare interpretations' are all text level objectives. The activities in this unit will further develop your ability to compare and evaluate different viewpoints and interpretations to arrive at your own considered viewpoint. The text you are studying is, of course, a play. You will be asked to make decisions about how you would present extracts from scenes to help you to consider the play as a performance. This drama and discussion work will help you to respond in a balanced way when you write an essay in timed conditions.

In section B of the test you will be asked to write about two extracts from the play you have studied. The question will focus on one or more of the key aspects of the extracts: character and motivation; language; themes, issues and ideas; and the play in performance. You will be expected to refer closely to the extracts and provide evidence to support your views.

In the first part of this unit, you will be developing relevant skills by looking closely at extracts from plays which are not usually set for study in the Key Stage 3 tests: *The Merchant of Venice* and *The Winter's Tale*. Later, you will be considering a text that is frequently studied in Key Stage 3: *Macbeth*.

Actors rehearsing a play.

English Works

Exploring scenes from Shakespeare

The Merchant of Venice

Shylock, a Jewish money-lender, loans Antonio, a merchant, some money, on the understanding that if the money is not repaid in time, Shylock will have a 'pound of Antonio's flesh' in compensation. Antonio's fleet is sunk and he is unable to repay the money, so he claims his 'bond' (the flesh!). A trial is held where Portia successfully defends Antonio and consequently Shylock is left a broken man.

TASK

This first task will help you remember some of the techniques used by Shakespeare in his plays:

❶ Working in pairs, look closely at the set of cards provided. For each technique card, you need to find a matching quotation. There may be more than one possible answer!
❷ Discuss *the impact* on the audience of at least three of these techniques.
❸ Report back to the rest of the class.

Act 3 Scene 1

You are now going to read and discuss the opening part of Act 3, where two of Antonio's friends, Solanio and Salerio, are talking about one of Antonio's ships that has been wrecked. Shylock enters and gives a heartfelt account of why he will pursue his 'bond' if Antonio is unable to repay his loan.

Sol.	Let me say "amen" betimes, lest the devil cross my prayer, for here he comes in the likeness of a Jew. 20	*betimes*: immediately
	Enter SHYLOCK.	
	How now Shylock! what news among the merchants?	
Shy.	You knew, none so well, none so well as you, of my daughter's flight.	
Sal.	That's certain,—I (for my part) knew the tailor that made the wings she flew withal. 25	*withal*: with
Sol.	And Shylock (for his own part) knew the bird was fledge, and then it is the complexion of them all to leave the dam.	*fledge*: fledged, having grown feathers on its wings
		dam: mother
Shy.	She is damn'd for it.	

English Works 83

Sal. That's certain, if the devil may be her judge. 30
Shy. My own flesh and blood to rebel!
Sol. Out upon it old carrion! rebels it at these years?
Shy. I say my daughter is my flesh and my blood.
Sal. There is more difference between thy flesh and hers, than between jet and ivory, more between your 35 bloods, than there is between red wine and Rhenish: but tell us, do you hear whether Antonio have had any loss at sea or no?
Shy. There I have another bad match, a bankrupt, a prodigal, who dare scarce show his head on the Rialto, 40 a beggar that was us'd to come so smug upon the mart: let him look to his bond! he was wont to call me usurer, let him look to his bond! he was wont to lend money for a Christian cur'sy, let him look to his bond!
Sal. Why I am sure if he forfeit, thou wilt not take his 45 flesh,—what's that good for?
Shy. To bait fish withal,—if it will feed nothing else, it will feed my revenge; he hath disgrac'd me, and hind'red me half a million, laugh'd at my losses, mock'd at my gains, scorned my nation, thwarted 50 my bargains, cooled my friends, heated mine enemies,—and what's his reason? I am a Jew. Hath not a Jew eyes? hath not a Jew hands, organs, dimensions, senses, affections, passions? fed with the same food, hurt with the same weapons, subject to the 55 same diseases, healed by the same means, warmed and cooled by the same winter and summer as a Christian is?—if you prick us do we not bleed? if you tickle us do we not laugh? if you poison us do we not die? and if you wrong us shall we not revenge?— 60 if we are like you in the rest, we will resemble you in that. If a Jew wrong a Christian, what is his humility? revenge! If a Christian wrong a Jew, what should his sufferance be by Christian example?—why revenge! The villainy you teach me I will execute, and it shall 65 go hard but I will better the instruction.

---

the devil: i.e. Shylock himself

Out ... carrion: you dirty old man

Rhenish: expensive white German wine

match: bargain

mart: stock exchange, the Rialto

hindered ... million: prevented me from making half a million (ducats) profit

bargains: business deals

dimensions: parts of the body

what is his humility: what does the Christian (who ought to bear his sufferings with humility) do?

what ... be: how should he endure it?

it shall ... instruction: if you are not very careful, I shall do even more harm than you have taught me to do

Exploring scenes from Shakespeare

❶ Working in groups, re-read and discuss Shylock's long speech. Focus on the following questions:
  ❑ What are the key ideas in this speech?
  ❑ How has Shakespeare conveyed Shylock's feelings? Think carefully about the dramatic impact of both the language and techniques used.

Remember that for each point you make, you need to find evidence from the text to support your ideas.

❷ Record your findings in a copy of the table below. For guidance, one example has already been completed.

Line(s)	Key ideas	Quotation	Techniques used	Dramatic impact
47–48	Desire for revenge	'…if it will feed nothing else, it will feed my revenge'	prose	– an informal conversation, which contrasts with the status and formality of the palace and trial scenes, so the prose is appropriate
			repetition	– repetition of 'feed' emphasises Shylock's bitterness and strong desire for revenge
			personification	– it's as though his revenge has taken on a life of its own: it's dominating his thoughts, and even, perhaps, consuming him/his reason

TASK

❶ From your work on the play so far, discuss whether you think Shylock is a villain or victim and why. Remember to support your ideas with evidence from the text.

❷ What issues does the presentation of Shylock raise for audiences in the twenty-first century?

English Works

Act 4 Scene 1

You are now going to read and possibly watch the trial scene and then focus in on some of the views presented by the different characters. The Duke's court has gathered to hear evidence from Shylock, who is in court alone, and Antonio, who is supported by his friends and defended by Portia.

[ACT IV]
[SCENE I.—*Venice. A Court of Justice.*]

Enter the DUKE, *the Magnificoes,* ANTONIO, BASSANIO, GRATIANO, SALERIO *and others*.

Duke.	What, is Antonio here?	
Ant.	Ready, so please your grace!	
Duke.	I am sorry for thee,—thou art come to answer	
	A stony adversary, an inhuman wretch,	
	Uncapable of pity, void, and empty	5
	From any dram of mercy.	
Ant.	I have heard	
	Your grace hath ta'en great pains to qualify	
	His rigorous course; but since he stands obdurate,	
	And that no lawful means can carry me	
	Out of his envy's reach, I do oppose	10
	My patience to his fury, and am arm'd	
	To suffer with a quietness of spirit,	
	The very tyranny and rage of his.	
Duke.	Go one and call the Jew into the court.	
Sal.	He is ready at the door,—he comes my lord.	15

Enter SHYLOCK.

Duke.	Make room, and let him stand before our face.	
	Shylock the world thinks, and I think so too,	
	That thou but leadest this fashion of thy malice	
	To the last hour of act, and then 'tis thought	
	Thou'lt show thy mercy and remorse more strange	20
	Than is thy strange apparent cruelty;	
	And where thou now exacts'st the penalty,	
	Which is a pound of this poor merchant's flesh,	
	Thou wilt not only loose the forfeiture,	
	But touch'd with human gentleness and love,	25
	Forgive a moiety of the principal,	
	Glancing an eye of pity on his losses	
	That have of late so huddled on his back,	
	Enow to press a royal merchant down,	
	And pluck commiseration of his state	30
	From brassy bosoms and rough hearts of flint,	
	From stubborn Turks, and Tartars never train'd	
	To offices of tender courtesy:	
	We all expect a gentle answer Jew!	
Shy.	I have possess'd your grace of what I purpose,	35
	And by our holy Sabbath have I sworn	
	To have the due and forfeit of my bond,—	
	If you deny it, let the danger light	
	Upon your charter and your city's freedom!	

thou … act: you intend to carry on with this show of cruelty until the last moment

exact'st: insist on having

Forgive … principal: allow him to keep a part of the original sum he borrowed

loose the forefeiture: refuse to accept the penalty that Antonio should pay

Enow: enough

commiseration of: sympathy for

stubborn: unfeeling

possess'd: informed

light: descend

due … bond: the proper penalty for not repaying my loan

English Works

Exploring scenes from Shakespeare

	You'll ask me why I rather choose to have	40
	A weight of carrion flesh, than to receive	
	Three thousand ducats: I'll not answer that!	
	But say it is my humour,—is it answer'd?	
	What if my house be troubled with a rat,	
ban'd: poisoned	And I be pleas'd to give ten thousand ducats	45
	To have it ban'd? what, are you answer'd yet?	
	Some men there are love not a gaping pig!	
	Some that are mad if they behold a cat!	
	And others when the bagpipe sings i'th'nose,	
	Cannot contain their urine—for affection	50
	(Master of passion) sways it to the mood	
	Of what it likes or loathes,—now for your answer:	
	As there is no firm reason to be rend'red	
	Why he cannot abide a gaping pig,	
	Why he a harmless necessary cat,	55
	Why he a woollen bagpipe, but of force	
	Must yield to such inevitable shame,	
	As to offend himself being offended:	
	So can I give no reason, nor I will not,	
lodg'd: deep-rooted	More than a lodg'd hate, and a certain loathing	60
	I bear Antonio, that I follow thus	
	A losing suit against him!—are you answered?	
Bass.	This is no answer thou unfeeling man,	
	To excuse the current of thy cruelty.	
Shy.	I am not bound to please thee with my answers!	65
Bass.	Do all men kill the things they do not love?	
Shy.	Hates any man the thing he would not kill?	
Bass.	Every offence is not a hate at first!	
Shy.	What! wouldst thou have a serpent sting thee twice?	
Ant.	I pray you think you question with the Jew,—	70
	You may as well go stand upon the beach	
bate: reduce	And bid the main flood bate his usual height,	
	You may as well use question with the wolf,	
	Why he hath made the ewe bleak for the lamb:	
	You may as well forbid the mountain pines	75
	To wag their high tops, and to make no noise	
	When they are fretten with the gusts of heaven:	
	You may as well do any thing most hard	
	As seek to soften that—than which what's harder?—	
	His Jewish heart! Therefore (I do beseech you)	80
	Make no moe offers, use no farther means,	
	But with all brief and plain conveniency	
	Let me have judgment, and the Jew his will!	
Bass.	For thy three thousand ducats here is six!	
Shy.	If every ducat in six thousand ducats	85
	Were in six parts, and every part a ducat,	
	I would not draw them, I would have my bond!	
Duke.	How shalt thou hope for mercy rend'ring none?	
Shy.	What judgment shall I dread doing no wrong?	
	You have among you many a purchas'd slave,	90
	Which (like your asses, and your dogs and mules)	
	You use in abject and in slavish parts,	
	Because you bought them,—shall I say to you,	
	Let them be free, marry them to your heirs?	

carrion: rotten

it is my humour: because I want it

a gaping pig: a pig's head, roasted, with the mouth open

affection ... loathes: prejudice is stronger than any emotion (passion), and directs over emotion to love or hate the objects of our prejudice

but ... offended: but when he is himself offended, he is compelled to react in in such a shameful way that he must give offence to others

a losing suit: a legal case where I must lose money

current: outpouring

Every ... at first: a single offence is not cause for hatred

think ... Jew: remember that you are arguing with the Jew

wag: wave

fretten: blown

draw: accept

in abject ... parts: for lowly and servile tasks

English Works 87

	Why sweat they under burthens? let their beds	95	*Be season'd … viands*: be treated with same food as your own
	Be made as soft as yours, and let their palates		
	Be season'd with such viands? you will answer		
	"The slaves are ours,"—so do I answer you:		
	The pound of flesh which I demand of him		
	Is dearly bought, 'tis mine and I will have it:	100	
fie: shame	If you deny me, fie upon your law!		
	There is no force in the decrees of Venice:		*force*: power
	I stand for judgment,—answer, shall I have it?		

        * * *

Por.	Is your name Shylock?		
Shy.	Shylock is my name.	175	
Por.	Of a strange nature is the suit you follow,		
	Yet in such rule, that the Venetian law		*in such rule*: so correctly
	Cannot impugn you as you do proceed.		
	You stand within his danger, do you not?		
Ant.	Ay, so he says.		
Por.	Do you confess the bond?		
Ant.	I do.		
Por.	Then must the Jew be merciful.	180	
Shy.	On what compulsion must I? tell me that.		
Por.	The quality of mercy is not strain'd,		*is not strain'd*: cannot be forced
	It droppeth as the gentle rain from heaven		
	Upon the place beneath: it is twice blest,		
	It blesseth him that gives, and him that takes,	185	
becomes: suits	'Tis mightiest in the mightiest, it becomes		
	The throned monarch better than his crown.		
	His sceptre shows the force of temporal power,		The King's sceptre symbolises his earthly ('temporal') power, which is the proper characteristic ('attribute') of a royal man ('majesty') who commands respect ('awe')
	The attribute to awe and majesty,		
	Wherein doth sit the dread and fear of kings:	190	
	But mercy is above this sceptred sway,		
	It is enthroned in the hearts of kings,		
	It is an attribute to God himself;		
	And earthly power doth then show likest God's		*seasons*: moderates
	When mercy seasons justice: therefore Jew,	195	
	Though justice be thy plea, consider this,		*in … salvation*: if we were all to get what we deserve, in the strict course of justice none of us would be saved
	That in the course of justice, none of us		
	Should see salvation: we do pray for mercy,		
	And that same prayer, doth teach us all to render		
	The deeds of mercy. I have spoke thus much	200	
	To mitigate the justice of thy plea,		*To mitigate … plea*: To ask you to soften your demand for justice
	Which if thou follow, this strict court of Venice		
	Must needs give sentence 'gainst the merchant there.		
Shy.	My deeds upon my head! I crave the law,	*discharge*: repay	*My … head*: I will take the responsibility for what I am doing
	The penalty and forfeit of my bond.	205	
Por.	Is he not able to discharge the money?		
Bass.	Yes, here I tender it for him in the court,	*tender*: offer	
	Yea, twice the sum,—if that will not suffice,		
be bound: make a legal promise	I will be bound to pay it ten times o'er		
	On forfeit of my hands, my head, my heart,—	210	
	If this will not suffice, it must appear		
	That malice bears down truth. And I beseech you		*bears down*: overcomes
wrest: twist	Wrest once the law to your authority,—		
	To do a great right, do a little wrong,—		*once*: on this one occasion
curb: restrain	And curb this cruel devil of his will.		

Exploring scenes from Shakespeare

TASK

1. Working in small groups, discuss the **views and ideas presented by the different characters** in this opening section of the trial scene and the **dramatic impact** these speeches are likely to have on the audience. Remember that Shylock, a Jew, is being tried in a Christian court.
2. Record your comments in a copy of the grid below. The first row has already been completed as an example:

Character	Views expressed	Dramatic impact
The Duke	– Shylock is likely to show mercy at the last minute (lines 17–21) – He feels sympathy for Antonio: 'poor merchant' and 'pluck commiseration of his state' – He seems to almost command Shylock to forgive Antonio	– Considering the Duke's status and authority, it seems as though Shylock is in the wrong and everyone is sympathetic to Antonio. His views would echo what many people in the audience feel and would serve to reinforce their prejudgements about Shylock. – Audiences at the time would have been swept along/sympathetic to this view. Modern audiences would probably query whether it is possible for Shylock to have a fair trial.
Antonio		
Bassanio		
Shylock		
Portia		

TASK

Further discuss the question: Is Shylock a villain or a victim? Have your views about Shylock changed as a result of studying the court scene? Focus especially on the ways in which Shylock has been presented to the audience. What factors may have caused you to modify your views?

English Works

The Winter's Tale

Leontes, King of Sicilia, suddenly suffers from an acute sense of jealousy and suspicion, and becomes convinced that Hermione, his wife, had an affair with Polixenes, Leontes' friend. He falsely accuses her of this, and at her trial condemns her. Hermione collapses and then 'dies'. Leontes immediately realises the consequences of his irrational jealousy. He suffers for 16 years before Paulina, his loyal servant, shows him Hermione's statue, which then 'comes to life'. At the end of the play Leontes is reconciled with Hermione.

TASK

You are about to look closely at some lines from the play. They are all spoken by Leontes, King of Sicilia, at the start of Act 2 of the play. His friend, Polixenes, has run away from Leontes' court after hearing that Leontes had accused him of having an affair with Hermione, Leontes' wife. Camillo, Leontes' servant, had helped Polixenes to escape.

1. Working in a small group, read your lines out loud.
2. Discuss what you can deduce about **character** and/or **theme**.
3. Discuss the language and techniques Shakespeare has used. How do they add to the dramatic impact of the lines?
4. Report your findings back to the rest of the class.

Act 3 Scene 2

Now read the trial scene: Leontes has placed Hermione on trial for adultery.

Scene 2

Enter Leontes, Lords, *and* Officers

Leontes
This sessions, to our great grief we pronounce,
Even pushes 'gainst our heart: the party tried
The daughter of a king, our wife, and one
Of us too much belov'd. Let us be clear'd
Of being tyrannous, since we so openly   5
Proceed in justice, which shall have due course,
Even to the guilt or the purgation.
Produce the prisoner.

* * *

sessions: trial
tried: to be tried
purgation: acquittal
Even ... heart: strikes right to my heart
openly: publicly
have due course: be carried out in the proper manner

Exploring scenes from Shakespeare

Hermione
Sir,
You speak a language that I understand not.
My life stands in the level of your dreams, 80
Which I'll lay down.
Leontes
                    Your actions are my dreams.
You had a bastard by Polixenes,
And I but dream'd it. As you were past all shame—
Those of your fact are so—so past all truth;
Which to deny concerns more than avails: for as 85
Thy brat hath been cast out, like to itself,
No father owning it—which is indeed
More criminal in thee than it—so thou
Shalt feel our justice, in whose easiest passage
Look for no less than death. 90
Hermione
                    Sir, spare your threats!
The bug which you would fright me with I seek.
To me can life be no commodity:
The crown and comfort of my life, your favour,
I do give lost, for I do feel it gone,
But know not how it went. My second joy, 95
And first-fruits of my body, from his presence
I am barr'd, like one infectious. My third comfort,
Starr'd most unluckily, is from my breast—
The innocent milk in its most innocent mouth—
Hal'd out to murder. Myself on every post 100
Proclaim'd a strumpet; with immodest hatred
The childbed privilege denied, which 'longs
To women of all fashion; lastly, hurried
Here to this place, i'th'open air, before
I have got strength of limit. Now, my liege, 105
Tell me what blessings I have here alive
That I should fear to die. Therefore proceed.
But yet hear this—mistake me not: no life,
I prize it not a straw; but for mine honour,
Which I would free—if I shall be condemn'd 110
Upon surmises, all proofs sleeping else
But what your jealousies awake, I tell you
'Tis rigour and not law. Your honours all,
I do refer me to the oracle:
Apollo be my judge! 115

Margin glosses:

dreams: fantasies, delusions

Which ... avails: denying this is more trouble than it's worth

bug: bugbear, bogy

childbed privilege: the right to stay in bed for a period after giving birth

in the level: within the range

of your fact: guilty of your crime

for as ... death: just as your child has been treated like the outcast it is, with no father acknowledging it – and you are more guilty than the child in this – so you can't expect anything less than a death sentence for yourself from my judgement

commodity: advantage, enjoyment

give: account

Hal'd: dragged

longs: belongs

got ... limit: been given time to recover my strength

all ... else: since there's no other evidence

rigour and not law: tyranny and not justice

English Works

TASK

1. Working with the whole class, your teacher will show you how to read closely and analyse a short extract from the court scene.
2. Working in a small group, analyse the ways in which Leontes and Hermione have been presented in the rest of the scene. What do you find out about each character? What techniques are used to convey their character to the audience? You may wish to highlight and annotate a copy of the scene.
3. Report your findings to the rest of the class.

Act 5 Scene 3

You are now going to watch and read the final scene of the play and then consider some of the views of Leontes presented by the other characters at this point in the play. Leontes, members of his family (his daughter, Perdita, and her husband, Florizel, who is also Polixenes' son), Polixenes, and Leontes' loyal courtier, Camillo, have all come to see Hermione's 'statue', presented to them by Paulina.

> Paulina *draws a curtain and reveals*
> Hermione, *standing like a statue*
>
> **Paulina**
> I like your silence: it the more shows off
> Your wonder. But yet speak: first you, my liege.
> Comes it not something near?
> **Leontes**
>   Her natural posture!
> Chide me, dear stone, that I may say indeed
> Thou art Hermione; or rather, thou art she   25
> In thy not chiding, for she was as tender
> As infancy and grace. But yet, Paulina,
> Hermione was not so much wrinkled, nothing
> So aged as this seems.
> **Polixenes**
>   O, not by much!
> **Paulina**
> So much the more our carver's excellence,   30
> Which lets go by some sixteen years and makes her
> As she liv'd now.

English Works

Exploring scenes from Shakespeare

Leontes
                As now she might have done,
So much to my good comfort as it is
Now piercing to my soul. O, thus she stood,
Even with such life of majesty—warm life,   35
As now it coldly stands—when first I woo'd her!
I am asham'd. Does not the stone rebuke me
For being more stone than it? O royal piece!

piece: work of art

There's magic in thy majesty, which has
My evils conjur'd to remembrance, and   40

My evils ... remembrance: brought to mind my offences

admiring: wondering

From thy admiring daughter took the spirits,
Standing like stone with thee.
Perdita
                      And give me leave,
And do not say 'tis superstition, that
I kneel and then implore her blessing. Lady,
Dear queen, that ended when I but began,   45
Give me that hand of yours to kiss!
Paulina
                      O, patience!
The statue is but newly fix'd, the colour's
Not dry.

The statue ... fix'd: the colours of the statue have only just been made fast

Camillo
My lord, your sorrow was too sore laid on,

sore: heavily, thickly

Which sixteen winters cannot blow away,   50
So many summers dry. Scarce any joy
Did ever so long live; no sorrow
But kill'd itself much sooner.
Polixenes
                    Dear my brother,
Let him that was the cause of this have power
To take off so much grief from you as he   55

Polixenes, identifying himself as the root cause of all the trouble, wants to take away some of Leontes' grief by sharing it

piece up: parcel, add up

Will piece up in himself.
Paulina
                Indeed, my lord,
If I had thought the sight of my poor image
Would thus have wrought you—for the stone is mine—

wrought: affected, moved

I'd not have show'd it.
Leontes
                Do not draw the curtain.

English Works   93

TASK

1. Discuss with the whole class the different views of Leontes presented in this final scene.
2. Working in a small group, compare how Leontes is presented in the first half of the play with how he is presented in this scene. Complete a copy of the following grid, including quotations to support your views.

Leontes' character, as presented in the first half of the play	Leontes' character, as presented in the final scene of the play
Jealous: 'Is whispering nothing? Is leaning cheek to cheek?'	
Arrogant: 'How blest am I/ In my just censure, in my true opinion!'	
Self-pitying: 'How accursed/ In being so blest!'	
Suspicious: 'There is a plot against my life, my crown. All's true that is mistrusted.'	
Cold/unfeeling towards Hermione: 'Produce the prisoner.'	
Harsh and accusatory: 'You had a bastard by Polixenes'	
Threatening: 'Look for no less than death.'	

TASK

1. Learn one short speech from any part of the play you have studied.
2. Working in a pair, take turns to present your speech to each other. Give each other advice, as a director, about how best to present the speech to an audience.
3. Report back on your ideas about the different techniques an actor may use when portraying a character on stage.
4. Working in pairs and using the ideas discussed, write the director's notes for one of your speeches. Below are some useful phrases:

> *Make sure you emphasise the word…in order to…, At this point, the actor's facial expression should suggest…, When you say line…, move towards…, Raise your voice to emphasise…, As the actor says line…, he should look towards…, Say line…in a…tone of voice so that…*

5. Present your director's notes and speech to the rest of the class.

English Works

Exploring scenes from Shakespeare

Macbeth

In the last part of the unit, you will study extracts from *Macbeth* and consider how plot, character and theme are developed in different, linked scenes.

Remember the plot?

> *Macbeth, tempted by his ambitious wife, the three witches and his own ambitions, murders King Duncan so that he may become the next King of Scotland. He then begins to remove anyone who stands in his way, eliminating first his true friend and confidante, Banquo. The witches had predicted that Banquo's children would be kings one day, not Macbeth's, and Macbeth is enraged by this. When the ghost of Banquo returns to plague Macbeth he decides to take even more desperate measures, visiting the witches and placing his future hopes on their ambiguous prophecies. He plans the annihilation of Macduff's family as a gesture of strength and defiance since Macduff and other Scottish lords seem to be turning against him. Clinging to the belief that he is invincible, since the prophecies seem to suggest no living man can defeat him, he rages alone against 10,000 English soldiers led by Duncan's son, Malcolm, and Macduff. The witches' treachery becomes apparent to him as he realises Fate has chosen Macduff to confront and defeat him. His wife already dead, Macbeth faces a bloody death alone and Malcolm becomes the next King of Scotland.*

Act 2 Scene 2

It is midnight, the 'witching hour', and Lady Macbeth awaits the return of her husband who is, as she speaks, murdering the sleeping King Duncan:

> Scene II. [*Macbeth's Castle.*]
> *Enter Lady* [*Macbeth*].
> **Lady Macbeth.** That which hath made them drunk hath made me bold;
> What hath quenched them hath given me fire. Hark! Peace!
> It was the owl that shrieked, the fatal bellman,
> Which gives the stern'st good-night. He is about it.
> The doors are open, and the surfeited grooms   5
> Do mock their charge with snores. I have drugged their possets,
> That death and nature do contend about them,
> Whether they live or die.
> **Macbeth.**   [*Within*] Who's there? What, ho?
> **Lady Macbeth.** Alack, I am afraid they have awaked
> And 'tis not done! Th' attempt and not the deed   10
> Confounds us. Hark! I laid their daggers ready;
> He could not miss 'em. Had he not resembled
> My father as he slept, I had done 't.
> *Enter Macbeth.*
>   My husband!

quenched: silenced, drugged

mock their charge: abandon their duties

fatal bellman: watchman who rang the bell before executions and burials

surfeited grooms: drunken servants

possets: hot drinks

English Works

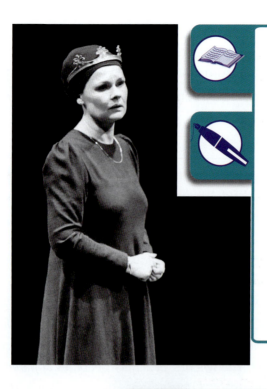

TASK

1. Working in pairs, read the above passage and identify the lines that show Lady Macbeth is excited, nervous and pleased with herself. It may be helpful to use a photocopy of the text and colour-code the lines that indicate each of these emotions.

2. Now write director's notes for this extract, explaining how the actress must use voice, gesture, facial expression and movement to provide maximum impact.

TASK

1. Read the passage opposite from later in the same scene.

2. Shakespeare has been careful to ensure that Lady Macbeth uses a variety of different types of sentence. These include sentences that begin with an imperative and questions. Working in small groups, re-read the passage and:
   ❏ identify the different sentence types used by Lady Macbeth at each point in her speech and their effect
   ❏ discuss why she makes such cruel comments about her husband. Why does she repeat the point about his cowardice? Do you think she realises the impact of such taunts on Macbeth?

English Works

Lady Macbeth. Who was it that thus cried? Why, worthy Thane,
You do unbend your noble strength, to think
So brainsickly of things. Go get some water, 45
And wash this filthy witness from your hand.
Why did you bring these daggers from the place?
They must lie there: go carry them, and smear
The sleepy grooms with blood.
Macbeth. I'll go no more.
I am afraid to think what I have done; 50
Look on 't again I dare not.
Lady Macbeth. Infirm of purpose!
Give me the daggers. The sleeping and the dead
Are but as pictures. 'Tis the eye of childhood
That fears a painted devil. If he do bleed,
I'll gild the faces of the grooms withal, 55
For it must seem their guilt.

Exit. Knock within.

Macbeth. Whence is that knocking?
How is 't with me, when every noise appalls me?
What hands are here? Ha! They pluck out mine eyes!
Will all great Neptune's ocean wash this blood
Clean from my hand? No; this my hand will rather 60
The multitudinous seas incarnadine,
Making the green one red.

Enter Lady [Macbeth].

Lady Macbeth. My hands are of your color, but I shame
To wear a heart so white. (*Knock.*) I hear a knocking
At the south entry. Retire we to our chamber. 65
A little water clears us of this deed:
How easy is it then! Your constancy
Hath left you unattended. (*Knock.*) Hark! more knocking.
Get on your nightgown, lest occasion call us
And show us to be watchers. Be not lost 70
So poorly in your thoughts.
Macbeth. To know my deed, 'twere best not know myself. (*Knock.*)
Wake Duncan with thy knocking! I would thou couldst!

Exeunt.

---

unbend: relax, weaken

grooms: servants, bodyguards

gild: paint with blood (a pun on gild/guilt)

withal: with it (blood)

Neptune: god of the sea

incarnadine: make blood-red

your constancy … unattended: you've lost your nerve

Much of the tension in this scene is a result of the dramatic contrast between the reactions of the two characters to the murder. This is clearly demonstrated in their attitudes towards water.

TASK

Read and compare Macbeth's words in lines 60–62 with his wife's words in line 66. Present your ideas about their contrasting language and moods in a diagrammatic poster: would 'Power' (Lady Macbeth) and 'Paralysis' (Macbeth) be useful key words?

TASK

Next, you will be carrying out a role-play and mime. Drama is about enlarging or exaggerating normal experience, so your actions will need to be larger than life to have a strong impact on your audience.

❶ Working with a partner, decide on who will be A and B. Person A should perform the following actions to suggest great confidence/strength; person B should perform them to suggest paranoia/distress:

| Opening/reading a letter | waiting for a bus | pouring a drink | washing your hands |

❷ Now consider how you would advise the actress playing Lady Macbeth to do the first and last of these at different stages in the play.

Act 5 Scene 1

Next, you will read part of Act 5 Scene 1, and consider Lady Macbeth's changed fortunes and state of mind. She and her husband have achieved their ambition to become King and Queen of Scotland through a systematic process of murder, bribery and corruption. In this scene we see the great personal cost that she has had to bear; far from the happiness she expected, she is haunted by the past and is unable to sleep peacefully. In this scene her Nurse and a Doctor watch her sleepwalking:

English Works

Exploring scenes from Shakespeare

Doctor.	How came she by that light?	
Gentlewoman.	Why, it stood by her. She has light by her continually. 'Tis her command.	25
Doctor.	You see, her eyes are open.	
Gentlewoman.	Ay, but their sense are shut.	
Doctor.	What is it she does now? Look, how she rubs her hands.	30
Gentlewoman.	It is an accustomed action with her, to seem thus washing her hands: I have known her continue in this a quarter of an hour.	
Lady Macbeth.	Yet here's a spot.	
Doctor.	Hark! she speaks. I will set down what comes from her, to satisfy my remembrance the more strongly.	35
Lady Macbeth.	Out, damned spot! Out, I say! One: two: why, then 'tis time to do 't. Hell is murky. Fie, my lord, fie! A soldier, and afeard? What need we fear who knows it, when none can call our pow'r to accompt? Yet who would have thought the old man to have had so much blood in him?	40
Doctor.	Do you mark that?	
Lady Macbeth.	The Thane of Fife had a wife. Where is she now? What, will these hands ne'er be clean? No more o' that, my lord, no more o' that! You mar all with this starting.	45
Doctor.	Go to, go to! You have known what you should not.	50
Gentlewoman.	She has spoke what she should not, I am sure of that. Heaven knows what she has known.	
Lady Macbeth.	Here's the smell of the blood still. All the perfumes of Arabia will not sweeten this little hand. Oh, oh, oh!	55

seem: appear to be

You mar ... starting: you spoil everything with your nervousness

TASK

Working in a small group, consider how Lady Macbeth's character, behaviour, feelings and language are different in this scene, compared to Act 2 Scene 2. Remember for each comment, you need to give a quotation to support your ideas. Present your findings in a copy of the before and after chart below. The first point has already been filled in for you.

Before: Act 2 Scene 2	After: Act 5 Scene 1
Language: assertive; use of the imperative to indicate control and strength. Qualifying statements, with use of semi-colon, to show clear, calm thinking.	**Language:** disjointed, to reflect instability/ fragmented mind. Heavily punctuated and exclamatory sentences. Many questions, which convey her as helpless; she's lost her former strength. Repitition: 'Out… out' indicates her mind is trapped and going round in circles.

Having examined the dramatic effect of **character** in the play, your next focus is on the **theme** of leadership. There are several different leaders in the play, both constructive/ positive and destructive/negative, including Duncan, Malcolm and Edward the Confessor. Many of the characters discuss the qualities of a good leader – this subject was obviously of interest to Shakespeare himself – and they pass comment on Macbeth's style of leadership.

TASK

In pairs, re-read the following lines from the play, all spoken by or about Macbeth. Discuss:

- ❑ What images are used?
- ❑ What do they reveal about Macbeth's feelings at these key points?
- ❑ What impact do they have on the audience?

> I am in blood
> Stepp'd in so far, that, should I wade no more,
> Returning were as tedious as go o'er.
>
> *(Act 3:4, 136–138)*

Exploring scenes from Shakespeare

❚❚ O full of scorpions is my mind, dear wife ❚❚ *(Act 3:2, 36)*

❚❚ Now does he feel his title
Hang loose about him,
like a giant's robe
Upon a dwarfish thief. ❚❚ *(Act 5:2, 20–22)*

❚❚ They have tied me to a stake;
I cannot fly,
But bear-like I must fight
the course. ❚❚ *(Act 5:7, 1–2)*

Now re-read Act 3 Scene 2, lines 13–26:

Macbeth. We have scorched the snake, not killed it:
She'll close and be herself, whilst our poor malice
Remains in danger of her former tooth.   15
But let the frame of things disjoint, both the worlds suffer,
Ere we will eat our meal in fear, and sleep
In the affliction of these terrible dreams
That shake us nightly: better be with the dead,
Whom we, to gain our peace, have sent to peace,   20
Than on the torture of the mind to lie
In restless ecstasy. Duncan is in his grave;
After life's fitful fever he sleeps well.
Treason has done his worst: nor steel, nor poison,
Malice domestic, foreign levy, nothing,   25
Can touch him further.

close ... herself: join together again

poor malice: weak deeds (to gain the crown)

let the ... disjoint: let the universe shatter

Malice domestic: civil war

foreign levy: foreign armies

TASK

For each statement about Macbeth in the table below, find a quotation from this speech in Act 3 which reveals this quality. Complete a copy of the table below:

After the murds of Duncan what problems does Macbeth face as he tries to establish himself as King?	
Statement	Quotation
1. He lacks a strong power base	
2. Tough decisions lie ahead	
3. His personal life is affected by his worries	
4. He is haunted by the threat of assassination or treason	

English Works

TASK

① In pairs, look carefully at the extract below from Act 5 Scene 5 lines 9–28. This time, you need to agree appropriate statements about the problems faced by Macbeth and select quotations to support your views. Record your statements in a copy of the table that follows the extract, then report back to the class.

Macbeth. I have almost forgot the taste of fears:
The time has been, my senses would have cooled   10
To hear a night-shriek, and my fell of hair
Would at a dismal treatise rouse and stir
As life were in 't. I have supped full with horrors.
Direness, familiar to my slaughterous thoughts,
Cannot once start me.
           [*Enter Seyton.*]
             Wherefore was that cry?   15
Seyton. The Queen, my lord, is dead.
Macbeth. She should have died hereafter;
There would have been a time for such a word.
Tomorrow, and tomorrow, and tomorrow
Creeps in this petty pace from day to day,   20
To the last syllable of recorded time;
And all our yesterdays have lighted fools
The way to dusty death. Out, out, brief candle!
Life's but a walking shadow, a poor player
That struts and frets his hour upon the stage   25
And then is heard no more. It is a tale
Told by an idiot, full of sound and fury
Signifying nothing.

treatise: story

start: frighten

my fell of hair: every hair on my body

Direness: horror

Statement	Quotation
1. He has become hardened to pain and suffering	
2.	

TASK

In pairs, use hot seating to further explore Macbeth's character and the play's theme of leadership. One of you should be Macbeth and the other the interviewer. Note down some searching questions, focusing on Macbeth's reactions to his wife's death, the imminent attack by the English, his current and past leadership qualities, and other characters' style of leadership. Carry out the hot seating!

English Works

Exploring scenes from Shakespeare

TASK

Now answer the following test practice question:

In Act 3, Scene 2, lines 13–26 and Act 5, Scene 5, lines 9–28, what does the audience learn about Macbeth's development as a leader and how is this conveyed?

Remember:

- In the test you will have 45 minutes to answer a question like this. This includes planning, writing and editing time.
- Plan your essay quickly before you start. You will probably write between four and six paragraphs.
- Each paragraph should begin with a key point or topic sentence e.g. *The audience discovers in the first extract that…, In the second extract…, To sum up, the audience…*
- Use connectives within paragraphs to clarify your thinking for the reader e.g. *The audience also learns that…, Another example of…, Shakespeare uses… to …, The effect of this is to…*

To do well you will need to:

- Avoid retelling the story – focus on answering the question.
- Refer to both extracts and try to make connections.
- Refer closely to Shakespeare's language and techniques – and their effect!
- Include short quotations from the text to support your ideas. The two to four word mid-sentence quotation is particularly helpful in timed conditions e.g. *When Macbeth says he has 'supp'd full with horrors', it is clear that…*
- Explain the effect of quotations.
- Consider the dramatic impact of the extracts on an audience.
- Use formal language in your answer.

TASK

❶ Read the extract from a pupil's essay on the title you have just tackled.

❷ In pairs, discuss the strengths and weaknesses of the writing and decide whether the writer has heeded the advice given about how to produce an effective response. Then, report your findings back to the class.

❸ Bearing in mind the features of a good answer you have just identified, revise and improve your own essay.

English Works

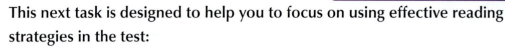

TASK

This next task is designed to help you to focus on using effective reading strategies in the test:

❶ Read, underline, annotate and colour-code the <u>photocopied</u> passages your teacher gives you from Act 1, Scenes 6 and 7. Focus on how Duncan's opinion of Macbeth and his castle is shown to be so different from the reality.

- ❑ Underline in one colour all the positive statements made about the castle by Duncan and Banquo. Number and annotate these.
- ❑ Using a different colour, underline the comments made by Macbeth and his wife in Act 1 Scene 7 that suggest the castle is far from a safe place. Again, number these and write brief notes alongside the text.
- ❑ Decide where Lady Macbeth is speaking with forced politeness in these scenes and where she is speaking the truth. Annotate the text with notes describing her behaviour.
- ❑ What is the dramatic effect for the audience of these scenes being next to one another? What is the atmosphere in each scene? How would you advise the actors to speak their lines?
- ❑ What impression of Duncan does the audience gain from these scenes?

❷ Report back. Agree on reading strategies which will be helpful in timed conditions.

English Works

UNIT 6 Taking a trip?

> Section 6 in Workbook - Finding and using information pages 24-29

KEY OBJECTIVES

In this unit you will learn about the following key objectives:

Synthesise information – combining information from different sources into one piece of writing and making sure it is written in a suitable way for the intended reader

Integrate information – combining a variety of information into a detailed account that 'hangs together' and is easily understood

Is there an attraction you'd like to visit? This unit focuses on family attractions in the UK that appeal to people interested in history, art, science or just having a good time! Attractions like the Tower of London and the Jorvik Viking Centre are visited by hundreds of thousands of people every year. Improved standards of living have led to an increase in people's leisure time and today's tourist industry generates a significant amount of wealth for the country.

In the first part of this unit you will be looking closely at website information about one of the UK's leading attractions before writing about it for a younger audience. In the second part you will be researching a further attraction by locating information in a variety of websites. You will decide which parts of the information would be of interest to 13–14 year olds when visiting this attraction. Finally, you will put the information together in a way that will be easy for your classmates to understand, in the form of a PowerPoint presentation.

This unit will help you develop skills that will be useful in all subjects: selecting information, taking notes, combining and organising information, and presenting information in an appropriate form and style.

English Works

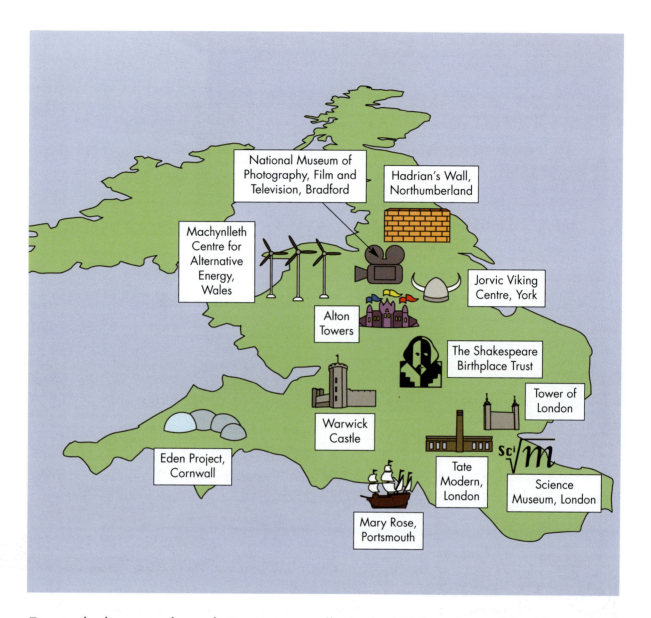

Due to the large numbers of attractions on offer in the UK there is considerable competition between them for customers. There are many places where you can find information about family attractions.

❶ With a partner, talk about family attractions you have visited and what makes a good one.

❷ Brainstorm ideas about where you could find information about an attraction. Report back to the class and consider how you would decide whether some sources are more reliable than others.

English Works

Taking a trip?

You are now going to be locating and selecting information about The Eden Project. This opened in 2001 and very quickly established itself as a top international attraction. In its first year it received almost 2 million visitors, 217,000 of whom were children. The Eden Project is home to plants from different countries, some housed in the largest glass domes in the world where the temperature and humidity can be controlled. The project tells visitors the story of how our relationship with plants is crucial to the future of the human race.

There are over 20 websites that provide information about The Eden Project. The purpose of most of these sites is to promote the project by encouraging people to visit. Some try to establish an image for the attraction that will appeal to certain types of people. Others provide information on a range of further attractions. The local tourist board runs a site seeking to persuade people to visit the region and go to Eden and other places of interest. There are even websites that have been designed by individuals as a result of their strong personal interest. Each of these websites has a specific audience in mind, including holidaymakers, families and people interested in supporting the project by keeping up to date with new developments.

You are now going to compare the two web pages (see pages 108–110). They are from two different Eden Project websites, and you will be considering their purpose and audience.

1. Read each web page with a partner.
2. Discuss the type of information included on each web page and the language used by the writers. What is the purpose of each website? At what type of audience is it aimed? Note your comments on a copy of the chart below:

	Purpose	How you know	Audience	How you know
Keith's Eden Project website				
Eden Project Cornwall Online				

English Works 107

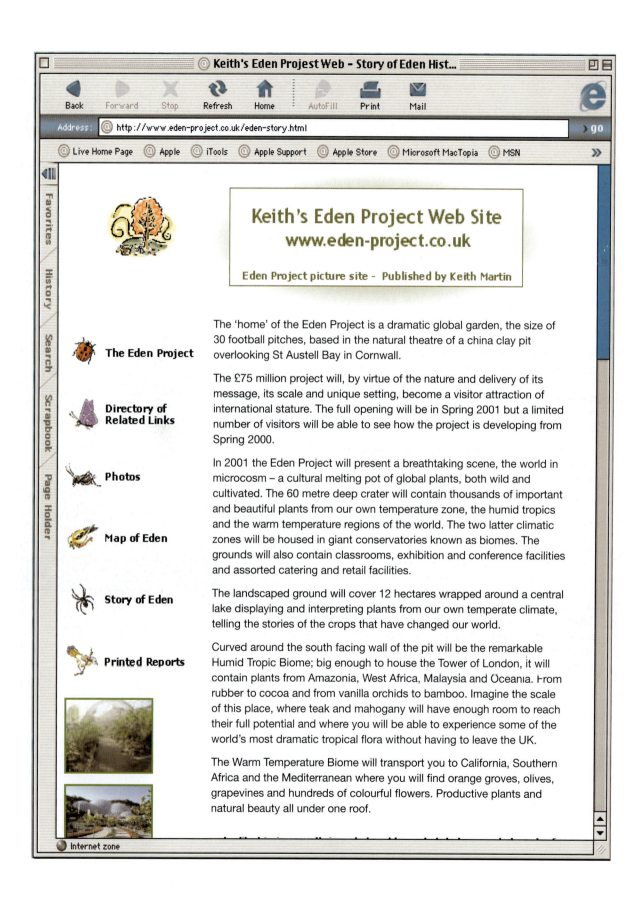

Taking a trip?

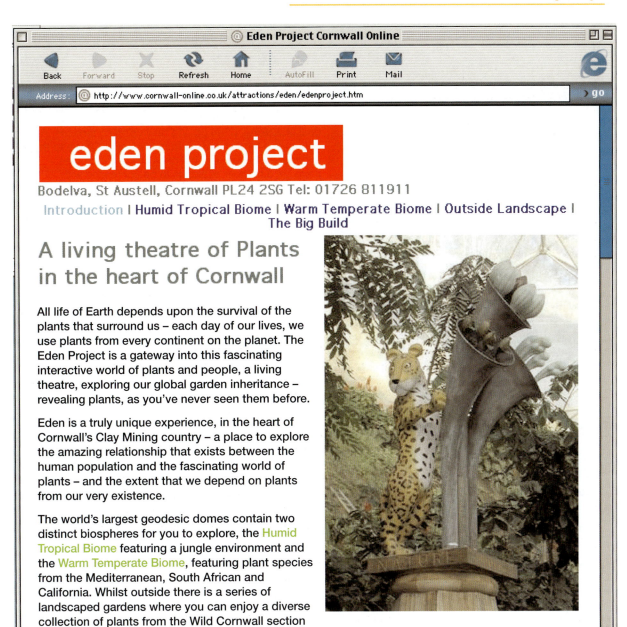

eden project

Bodelva, St Austell, Cornwall PL24 2SG Tel: 01726 811911

Introduction | Humid Tropical Biome | Warm Temperate Biome | Outside Landscape | The Big Build

A living theatre of Plants in the heart of Cornwall

All life of Earth depends upon the survival of the plants that surround us – each day of our lives, we use plants from every continent on the planet. The Eden Project is a gateway into this fascinating interactive world of plants and people, a living theatre, exploring our global garden inheritance – revealing plants, as you've never seen them before.

Eden is a truly unique experience, in the heart of Cornwall's Clay Mining country – a place to explore the amazing relationship that exists between the human population and the fascinating world of plants – and the extent that we depend on plants from our very existence.

The world's largest geodesic domes contain two distinct biospheres for you to explore, the Humid Tropical Biome featuring a jungle environment and the Warm Temperate Biome, featuring plant species from the Mediterranean, South African and California. Whilst outside there is a series of landscaped gardens where you can enjoy a diverse collection of plants from the Wild Cornwall section to the terraced tea slopes.

English Works

The Eden Project is very extensive, requiring a great deal of walking, often up and down sloping terraces. A train runs a regular service from the Visitor Centre to the entrance to the domes, but once inside the biomes there are a number of slopes to be contended with.

Comfortable shoes are strongly recommended. Once in the domes, you will immediately notice the change in humidity as you enter the Humid Tropical Biome, where temperatures reach 28° Centigrade – so regardless of the outside temperature, be warned that you will need a top layer of clothing that is easy to take off and easy to carry. Also on hot days, sun protection is also advisable (sun lotion and a hat) as the transparent ETFE film that the biomes are clad in, transmit UV light.

To enjoy your visit, plan to spend the whole day – there is so much to see; you need time to enjoy the site's true splendour. A visit to this dramatic and fascinating project will enable you to experience:

- A fantastic range of plants from around the world.
- Marvellous stores demonstrating the many ways in which man uses plants for: food, medicine, construction, entertainment, the air we breathe and a whole lot more.
- Information on the relationship between plants and the development of our global cultures.
- A glimpse into the future, following the use of plants in new designs and technologies.
- A chance to get involved: feeling, tasting, seeing, and using plants on themed tours and in a wide range of workshops.
- Demonstrations of resource use, and the showcasing of local and global projects and initiatives working towards securing a sustainable future.
- Information and simple practical ideas on how to care for the plants, and their habitats, that provide for us. Working towards a sustainable future.

Taking a trip?

You are now going to examine a page from the official website www.edenproject.com, endorsed by the registered charity that owns The Eden Project. The purpose of this page is to explain what the project stands for and contains a quotation from its director. A specific quote like this convinces us that we will be provided with the truth, as Tim Smit would be viewed as the leading expert on the project. With a wealth of information accessible to him, it is important that he selects key information and structures it in a helpful way. You are going to look at how the information provided is organised.

TASK

1. Read the page from www.edenproject.com below.
2. Using a copy of the web page, highlight any organisational techniques that have been used to structure the text. Annotate with comments about how different techniques help to orientate the reader. Look out for:
   - rhetorical questions
   - repetition
   - sub-headings
   - topic sentences
   - paragraphs
   - any other features

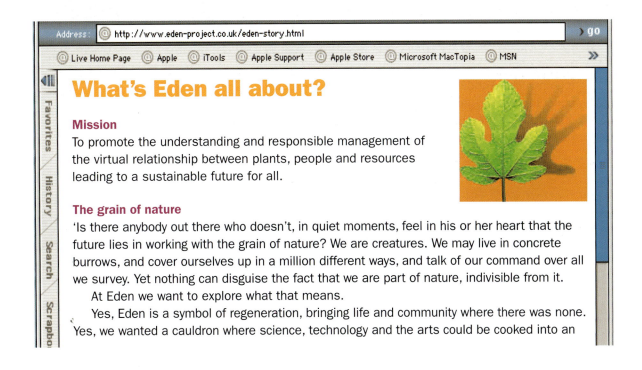

What's Eden all about?

Mission
To promote the understanding and responsible management of the virtual relationship between plants, people and resources leading to a sustainable future for all.

The grain of nature
'Is there anybody out there who doesn't, in quiet moments, feel in his or her heart that the future lies in working with the grain of nature? We are creatures. We may live in concrete burrows, and cover ourselves up in a million different ways, and talk of our command over all we survey. Yet nothing can disguise the fact that we are part of nature, indivisible from it.
    At Eden we want to explore what that means.
    Yes, Eden is a symbol of regeneration, bringing life and community where there was none.
Yes, we wanted a cauldron where science, technology and the arts could be cooked into an

English Works

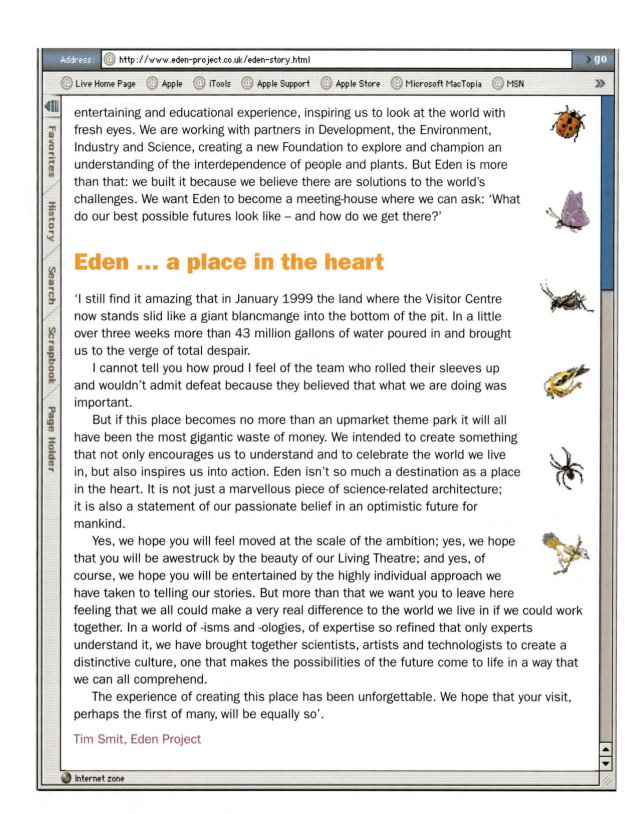

entertaining and educational experience, inspiring us to look at the world with fresh eyes. We are working with partners in Development, the Environment, Industry and Science, creating a new Foundation to explore and champion an understanding of the interdependence of people and plants. But Eden is more than that: we built it because we believe there are solutions to the world's challenges. We want Eden to become a meeting-house where we can ask: 'What do our best possible futures look like – and how do we get there?'

Eden ... a place in the heart

'I still find it amazing that in January 1999 the land where the Visitor Centre now stands slid like a giant blancmange into the bottom of the pit. In a little over three weeks more than 43 million gallons of water poured in and brought us to the verge of total despair.

I cannot tell you how proud I feel of the team who rolled their sleeves up and wouldn't admit defeat because they believed that what we are doing was important.

But if this place becomes no more than an upmarket theme park it will all have been the most gigantic waste of money. We intended to create something that not only encourages us to understand and to celebrate the world we live in, but also inspires us into action. Eden isn't so much a destination as a place in the heart. It is not just a marvellous piece of science-related architecture; it is also a statement of our passionate belief in an optimistic future for mankind.

Yes, we hope you will feel moved at the scale of the ambition; yes, we hope that you will be awestruck by the beauty of our Living Theatre; and yes, of course, we hope you will be entertained by the highly individual approach we have taken to telling our stories. But more than that we want you to leave here feeling that we all could make a very real difference to the world we live in if we could work together. In a world of -isms and -ologies, of expertise so refined that only experts understand it, we have brought together scientists, artists and technologists to create a distinctive culture, one that makes the possibilities of the future come to life in a way that we can all comprehend.

The experience of creating this place has been unforgettable. We hope that your visit, perhaps the first of many, will be equally so'.

Tim Smit, Eden Project

Taking a trip?

Many of the websites on The Eden Project are designed to persuade people to visit and of course the language plays a crucial role. There are many persuasive techniques that can be exploited. For example, writing in the second person involves the reader in the experience; emotive language can suggest how exciting the visit would be; repetition and alliteration emphasise key points; and figurative language can bring ideas to life.

TASK

1. Working in a pair, read the following web page from www.edenguide.co.uk.
2. Using a copy of the web page, highlight examples of different persuasive techniques used by the writer. Annotate with comments explaining their effect. Some of the annotations have already been done for you.

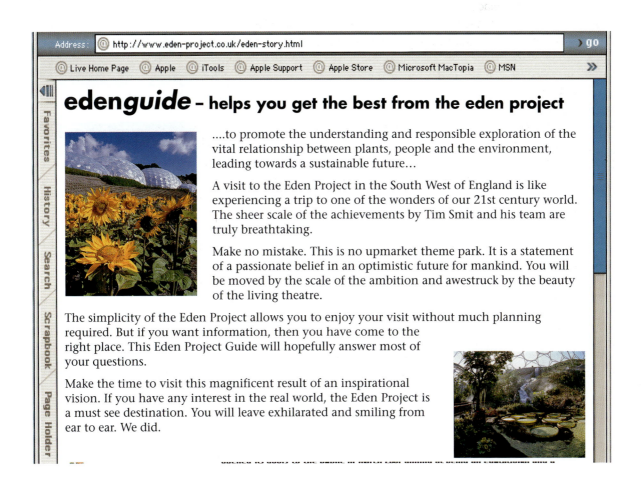

Address: http://www.eden-project.co.uk/eden-story.html

edenguide – helps you get the best from the eden project

....to promote the understanding and responsible exploration of the vital relationship between plants, people and the environment, leading towards a sustainable future…

A visit to the Eden Project in the South West of England is like experiencing a trip to one of the wonders of our 21st century world. The sheer scale of the achievements by Tim Smit and his team are truly breathtaking.

Make no mistake. This is no upmarket theme park. It is a statement of a passionate belief in an optimistic future for mankind. You will be moved by the scale of the ambition and awestruck by the beauty of the living theatre.

The simplicity of the Eden Project allows you to enjoy your visit without much planning required. But if you want information, then you have come to the right place. This Eden Project Guide will hopefully answer most of your questions.

Make the time to visit this magnificent result of an inspirational vision. If you have any interest in the real world, the Eden Project is a must see destination. You will leave exhilarated and smiling from ear to ear. We did.

English Works

By this stage in the unit you have learned a lot about different Eden Project websites: their different purposes and audiences, how they are structured and the language they use to persuade the reader. You will also know a lot about The Eden Project itself.

Every summer, local councils publish leaflets suggesting interesting family activities for the long school holiday. Renshire Council's 'Great Days Out' leaflet is aimed at 9–11 year olds and their parents, and is made available in primary schools. Its purpose is to encourage trips to interesting places. Each page describes how you could spend a day out at a particular attraction.

Your task is to gather relevant information from Eden Project websites then write a page about the project for 'Great Days Out' which will whet the appetites of children in Years 5 and 6.

1. In pairs, discuss the aspects of The Eden Project that will really interest your young readers.

2. Now start gathering relevant information from different Eden Project websites. Keep in mind your target audience – which features would 9–11 year olds enjoy most? Use a grid like the one below to note information:

Website	Interesting features for 9–11 year old visitors
1. Eden Project Cornwall Online	– Humid Tropical Biome which contains jungle environment
2.	

English Works

Taking a trip?

 TASK continued

❸ Renshire Council requires each page of 'Great Days Out' to have a similar format: a description of the main things to see and do over the course of your day visit. Use a copy of the timetable below to plan a good day out at The Eden Project, incorporating all the interesting features you have already noted:

Time	Things to do
10.00	Arrive at Visitor Centre and look round
10.30	Take train to domes
11.00	Visit Humid Tropical Biome first. See…
1.00	

❹ Now write your page for 'Great Days Out', describing a good day out at The Eden Project. Make use of the advice below:

Advice

1) Write in continuous prose and divide your work into paragraphs.
2) Use the timetable you have devised to organise your description of the day. You could have a paragraph on each of the following:

- An explanation of The Eden Project
- What to do in the morning
- Where to eat
- What to do in the afternoon
- What you will gain from a visit

English Works 115

3) Think carefully about how you will make sure the text is coherent for your 9–11 year old readers. Signpost the text so they can follow their way through it without getting lost. The beginning of paragraphs is particularly important. Start paragraphs with phrases like:

'The Eden Project is one of the...'
'When you arrive you will want to...'
'In the morning, why not visit...'
'At lunchtime you may...'
'Why not start the afternoon by...'
'Finally, make sure you don't miss...'
'By the end of the day, you will have...'

4) Make sure you write in a way that will interest your reader. Try some of the following techniques:

- Vary the kind of sentences you use
- Refer to the reader e.g. 'If you're interested in the environment and countries around the world then The Eden Project is a must visit'
- Include a rhetorical question e.g. 'Have you ever thought of how exciting it would be to explore a real jungle?'
- Use imperative verbs at the start of sentences e.g. 'Persuade someone to take you to the West Country so that you can...'
- Use a lively, friendly style that will gain the attention of 9–11 year olds e.g. 'You'll be wowed by the project' or 'You too can have a go at being a surf dude'

English Works

So far you have been looking closely at different sources of information about just one tourist attraction. In the next part of this unit you are going to work in groups on researching different tourist attractions. After you have gathered information about your chosen attraction from relevant websites, you will design a PowerPoint presentation about it. Your audience will be the rest of the class and its purpose will be to give them information about the attraction and convince them that it would be worth a visit.

So what exactly is a PowerPoint presentation? As you will probably know, it is a computer programme that allows you to prepare and present information to an audience, with all the advantages of modern technology. When using PowerPoint, the first stage is to plan and prepare a sequence of 'slides' about the chosen subject. These are likely to contain written information but various visual and sound effects can also be incorporated. The completed slides can then be projected, one by one, to an audience and the presenter can add spoken comments to complement them. Below are two typical slides from a PowerPoint presentation:

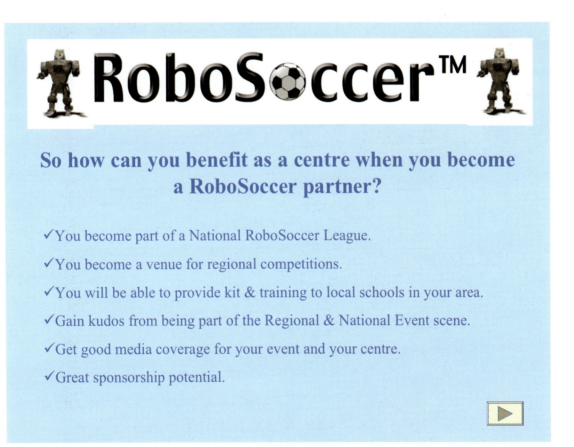

One page from a PowerPoint presentation about Robosoccer

Before you start preparing your own presentation, you need to think carefully about the specific features of this type of presentation.

TASK

1. In a pair, discuss who is most likely to use a PowerPoint presentation and for what purpose. Report back to the rest of the class.
2. Watch the sample PowerPoint presentation. Note the different features that have been included, for example its use of headings, background colour, sound. Was it clearly structured? Was it interesting?
3. What was the purpose of this PowerPoint presentation? Who was the intended audience? How do you know?
4. What do you think are the advantages/disadvantages of a PowerPoint presentation compared with a conventional spoken presentation? Make notes on a copy of the grid below:

	Advantages	Disadvantages
PowerPoint		
Spoken presentation		

English Works

Taking a trip?

TASK

Working in a group of three or four, choose one of the attractions below that you would like to research:

Tate Modern **Tower of London** **Science Museum** **The Shakespeare Birthplace Trust**

Hadrian's Wall **Warwick Castle** **National Museum of Photography, Film and Television, Bradford**

❶ In your group, decide which search engine you will use to help you locate relevant information about your chosen attraction on the Internet e.g. Google, Alta Vista, Yahoo, Vivísimo. Agree on the key words you will use to help you find relevant information quickly e.g. Science Museum London.

❷ Look closely at several of the sites that your search engine has listed for you. Choose three that you think will be particularly useful to you.

❸ Select and note relevant information from the sites that you will be able to use in the PowerPoint presentation you will be producing. Remember you will need to provide your audience with information about the main features of the attraction. Use a copy of the following grid to help you organise your key points:

Location	
Opening times	
Cost	
Main features	
Facilities	
Other information	

English Works

To create an effective PowerPoint presentation you will need to organise the information you have noted into a series of slides. Remember your aim is to provide the audience with a coherent account of the main features of your attraction but also explain why it will appeal to the pupils in your class.

You will need to plan a clear sequence of slides so that your audience does not get confused. The first few slides in your presentation will need to orientate the audience and provide practical information e.g. where the attraction is and how much it costs to get in. You will then need to explain the main features of the attraction: this may need two or three slides. Finally, you will need to explain why the attraction would interest Year 9 pupils and merit a visit. Your PowerPoint should include at least six slides.

Here is one example of how you could structure your presentation:

1. Name of attraction, location, its overall purpose.
2. Cost, opening times.
3. Main features on offer.
4. Further features.
5. Facilities e.g. cafe, interactive video.
6. How previous visitors have responded.
7. Practical information with Hyperlink to best website.
8. Your opinion of the attraction's potential appeal to 13–14 year olds.

❶ Look carefully at the notes you have taken about your attraction. Delete any material that you think will be inappropriate for your purpose and audience. Identify the main 'blocks' of information you have gathered.

❷ Use a copy of the grid opposite to plan what you will include in each of your slides. At this stage don't go into detail: concentrate on sequencing your 'blocks' of information.

English Works

Taking a trip?

Slide 1	Tate Modern on South Bank, London. Displays modern art.
Slide 2	
Slide 3	
Slide 4	
Slide 5	
Slide 6	
Slide 7	
Slide 8	

Once you are happy with your outlines for each slide and their sequence, you need to think about how to write each one in more detail. You will need to make decisions about the organisation of text on each slide, the language you use, and how to present your written information so that it is easy for the audience to digest.

TASK

Imagine that the person who produced the slide below has turned to you for advice on designing PowerPoint slides. Identify four or five features for them to work on and explain how to improve each one.

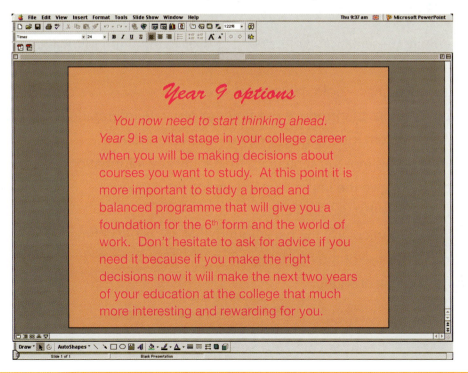

English Works

 Now look closely at the slide below. What do you think the designer of this slide has done well?

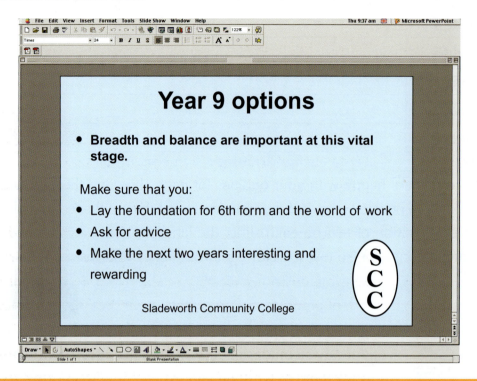

PowerPoint presentation writers need to bear in mind the following features:

1. Clear headings – bold, large point size.
2. Sub-headings to introduce examples or separate information.
3. Clear, modern font, large enough to read at a distance.
4. Bullet points (not full sentences) to identify key information.
5. Footers to give the impression of binding the sequence.
6. Illustrations that are appealing.
7. Colours, particularly the background, that are eye-catching but not too distracting.
8. Productive use of moving images.
9. Effective use of sound.

English Works

Taking a trip?

The next step is to write each slide. When you begin your presentation, you will need to make an immediate impact on your audience. You could open with a question or an impressive claim about your attraction. The slides in the middle of the presentation need to be clearly linked through headings and subheadings, so that the audience is guided through the information. Your final slide should sum up the presentation and stick in your audience's mind. The audience should feel convinced by your PowerPoint and keen to visit the attraction themselves.

TASK

1. Write each of your slides remembering that you are summing up key information in bullets and not writing in sentences. Make use of the positive features you identified earlier.
2. Now focus on the appearance and sound of your slides. Make sure each one is easily readable and has plenty of visual impact: make sensible decisions about type and size of font, colour of written text, use of graphics, colour of backgrounds. A moving image might appeal to your audience as well. Decide whether you wish to use music to create an appropriate mood, or sound effects to capture the audience's attention. Take care not to distract your audience from your purpose by including too many startling effects!

You're nearly there! Now you have completed your PowerPoint slides you need to think about what you are going to say about each one. You need to strike a careful balance. You don't want to say too much: after all, your audience can see the main information on screen. However, you will need to draw attention to key points, elaborate on information and make links between slides.

TASK

1. Using a printed notes version of your presentation, jot down comments alongside each slide, to remind you about what you are going to say about each one. You could incorporate some of the phrases on the following page to signpost new information:

English Works 123

'First of all it is extremely popular because…'

'In addition, it is possible to…'

'Many visitors claim that…'

'Most importantly, you must take advantage of…'

'As well as experiencing the… you can…'

'Overall you're guaranteed…'

Your slides	Your comments
Slide 1	_____
Slide 2	_____
Slide 3	_____

TASK

1. Rehearse your presentation in front of another group and ask them for constructive criticism. Try to be as natural as you can. The most common tendency is to rush what you are saying. Slow down to help the audience commit important points to memory and pause in certain places to indicate that you are moving on to something new. Make sure that you don't get fixated on your notes. With enough rehearsal time you should be able to establish eye contact with your audience and perhaps even smile! Vary your expression and consider how your tone could stir up enthusiasm. If you want to ensure that the audience is involved you could ask for comments during your presentation or provide an opportunity for questions at the end.
2. Make further improvements to your slides and spoken comments. After such thorough preparation you should now feel confident about the quality of your presentation.
3. Make your presentation to the rest of the class.

English Works

UNIT 7 Under your skin

In this unit you will learn about the following key objectives:

Layers of meaning – understanding how a writer's choice of words can have different meanings

Different cultural contexts – understanding how writers are influenced by where and how they live

This unit will get you thinking about the choices writers make about the words they use. We know that words are seldom neutral. Good writers will choose words carefully, making sure they are rich in meaning. Often they will work on more than one level. Good readers need to recognise these different layers of meaning.

angry   furious   indignant   *outraged*   *irate*

cross   *fuming*   riled   **annoyed**

seething   *irritated*

Writers are strongly influenced by the culture and traditions of where they live or where they were brought up as children. You will be considering how writers' backgrounds affect the decisions they make about language and style. This unit aims to broaden your understanding of writing from several different cultures, including South African, British/Caribbean and Jamaican.

The activities you carry out will help you prepare for your forthcoming GCSE English course. Over the next two years you will be required to look closely at a range of different kinds of text.

English Works

The texts in this unit include part of a story, poems and speeches. They all reveal something about the connection between culture and writing.

Culture can be defined as the common language, way of life, history, beliefs and knowledge of a particular group or society. It is the shared experience that shapes people's behaviour, values and traditions. Within any culture, there are specific **traditions** or **customs** that give expression to that culture. In South African culture, for example, communal cooking is very common; it is tradition that you share your food with guests or strangers who visit. From this has developed the modern barbecue, or *braaivleis*, during which ground mealie-meal and relish (*pap* and *sous*) is served as a filling accompaniment.

TASK

❶ In groups, discuss your own ideas about culture and tradition. What aspects of your culture are special to you? What traditions are important in your culture?

❷ In the same group, read through some of the following extracts. They are all comments from writers about their different cultures and how their sense of belonging to a particular group has helped shape their sense of identity.

Beverley Naidoo

I was born and brought up 'a Jo'burg girl', with the usual notions of most white South Africans, completely taking for granted our cook-cum-nanny, whose own children lived 300 kilometres away, cared for by… I don't know. She provided much of my actual mothering. We knew her as 'Mary'. I didn't know her real Tswana name. What I do recall, quite vividly, was how, when I was about eleven, she received a telegram and collapsed. Two of her three young daughters had died. It was diptheria – something for which I as a white child, had been vaccinated.

English Works

Under your skin

It was only years later that I began to realise the meaning of that scene. My education took place after I left school, not in any classroom. The early 1960s were a time of political ferment. Apartheid laws had stopped all but a few black students from attending my university. However, along with a small number of politically aware white students, they challenged my inability to see what was all around me. How was it that I had been so blind? It wasn't a time for sitting on the fence so I became involved in anti-apartheid activity, as my brother had done before me. In 1964 we were arrested along with a number of other activists and held in solitary confinement under the notorious '90 days law'. My brother spent almost three years in jail but I was a small fish and released after eight weeks. It was part of my education. After all, for black South Africans, the country itself was a vast jail.

Grace Nichols

When I'm in Guyana, or another part of the Caribbean – because I see myself as coming from the wider Caribbean also – I feel I belong there because I spring from that landscape. But partly because I have children in England, I also feel at home in this culture, with their dreams and aspirations. So I embrace both. England is where I live; where I make my living, but when I'm in England I'm always looking back. Both as a writer and as an individual, I'm always looking at both worlds.

Linton Kwesi Johnson

I do have a strong attachment to Jamaica. I'm living here (in England) for 33 years now but I do intend to retire in Jamaica… There's a new generation coming up (of black people in England) but I'm not sure that they're historically aware as my generation were. So there is that need to pass on to the next generation some institution building that my generation embarked upon. But I would like to contribute something to the land of my birth as well…

English Works

Roots Manuva

At the start you inevitably mimic your heroes. So when I started I copied an American accent.

Then he wised up to the fact that however hard he tried to copy them, he was never going to sound like Tupac or Ice T.

There was a British sensibility to whatever I did and I decided I had better work with it rather than against it.

So he rapped about cheese on toast and string vests – and suddenly found that he was at last being taken seriously.

Several writers also speak explicitly about their language choices, focusing on how they use a combination of Standard English and their own language (such as Jamaican or Creole) to create a more personal form of expression. This forms a vital part of how they explore and assert their individual identity. Choosing to write in their own dialect, for example, shows writers identifying with and celebrating their cultural roots. This is especially important for writers who no longer live in the country of their birth. It's a form of connecting with their past and the influences of their heritage. It's also through their own language that writers are able to give a strong voice to their concerns about injustices in their country. Both the following writers speak about language:

Bob Marley

Rastafari is a part of my historical heritage and a part of my cultural roots. Rasta has influenced Jamaican culture in a very big way. Not only in terms of the music but in terms of spirituality that it lent to reggae. Also in terms of the language, the Rastafari that has become a part of everyday Jamaican parlance... Rasta is important for me on that level – as a cultural force that broadened our consciousness and opened our consciousness to our African heritage and our African ancestry... what I've been doing with reggae poetry is to consolidate the rhythms of Caribbean speech, jazz rhythms, blues rhythms, calypso rhythms and so on.

English Works

Under your skin

Grace Nichols

As a writer and poet I'm excited by language, of course. I care about language, and maybe that's another reason why I write and continue to write. It's the battle with the language that I love. When it comes to writing poetry, it's the challenge of trying to create or chisel out a new language that I like. I like working in both Standard English and Creole. I tend to want to fuse the two tongues because I come from a background where the two worlds, Creole and Standard English, were constantly interacting, though Creole was regarded, obviously, as the inferior by the colonial powers when I was growing up and still has a social stigma attached to it in the Caribbean.

I think this is one of the main reasons why so many Caribbean poets, including myself, are now reclaiming our language heritage and exploring it. It's an act of spiritual survival on our part, the need (whether conscious or unconscious) to preserve something that's important to us. It's a language that our foremothers and forefathers struggled to create and we're saying that it's a valid, vibrant language. We're no longer going to treat it with contempt or allow it to be misplaced.

GLOSSARY

Some helpful definitions:

Dialect: a distinctive variation of a language with its own vocabulary and grammatical constructions. It is often used in a particular region or by people of a similar social or cultural background.

Creole: a language that has developed among people who did not share a common language and over time become the mother tongue of the community. Some creoles originated with the migration of slaves from Africa to America and the Caribbean, and the merging of the various languages spoken by the slaves and the colonial powers.

Standard English: the grammar and vocabulary of a dialect of English that has gained prestige and is now the most widely understood. It is used on the BBC news and taught in language schools around the world.

Heritage: anything from the past handed down by tradition e.g. customs, language.

English Works

TASK

❶ In your group, look carefully at the diagram below:

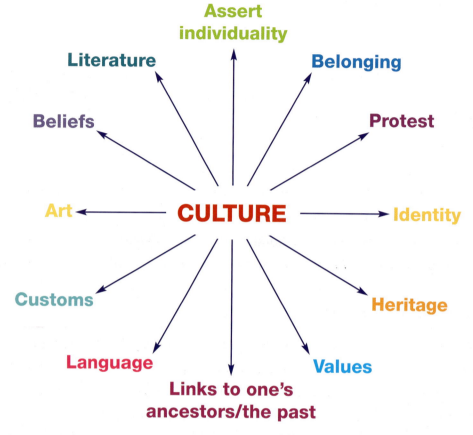

❷ Re-read the comments by the first four writers. Referring to the diagram for guidance, note the aspects of culture which are described by each writer. What exactly is each writer saying?

❸ Are there words or phrases that these writers have used which are particularly important or have a particular layer of meaning? Copy the grid below and note these words or phrases, explaining the meaning of each one.

Word or phrase	Meaning
'So I embrace both'	'embrace' suggests Grace Nichols feels attached to both Caribbean and English cultures.

❹ Report back to the rest of the class.

English Works

Under your skin

Focus on fiction

Next, you will study an extract from a short story set in South Africa, *Out of Bounds*, which was written by Beverley Naidoo in 2000.

In the story the writer explores how Rohan, a young Asian boy, is torn between two cultures: the more traditional and conservative views of his parents, and his experiences as a young child when he meets Solani, a black boy who needs his help. You will be looking closely at the language of the text to see how Beverley Naidoo presents this cultural conflict in her story.

TASK

❶ In pairs, discuss the title *Out of Bounds*. What does it suggest the story may be about?

❷ Report your views to the rest of the class.

Background to the extract

> Rohan's parents are annoyed when squatters, displaced as a result of the Mozambican floods, settle near their house. Rohan is forbidden any contact with these people, but he has noticed one boy in the camp who can make amazing model cars out of simple bits of wire. One day the boy, whose name is Solani, unexpectedly calls on Rohan to ask for water. His mother is having a baby and water is urgently needed. Should Rohan help the boy or respect his parents' wishes?
>
> In this extract, Rohan agrees to help Solani and to accompany him to the squatters' camp.

The bell rang just as he was getting interested in the first question. Nuisance! He hurried to the landing. If someone was standing right in front of the gate, it was possible to see who it was from the window above the stairs. He stood back, careful not to be seen himself. It was the same boy, an empty container on the ground each side of him! Didn't he know not to come to the house up here? But he was only a child and it looked as if he just wanted some water. It would be different if it were an adult or a complete stranger. Rohan's daydream also made him feel a little guilty. He could see the boy look anxiously through the bars, his hand raised as if wondering whether to ring the bell again. Usually when the boy was pushing his wire car on the way to school, he appeared relaxed and calm.

English Works

By the time the bell rang a second time, Rohan had decided. He hurried downstairs but slowed himself as he walked outside towards the gate.

'What do you want?' Rohan tried not to show that he recognised the boy.

'I need water for my mother. Please.' The boy held his palms out in front of him as if asking for a favour. 'My mother – she's having a baby – it's bad – there's no more water. Please.'

This was an emergency. Not on television but right in front of him. Still Rohan hesitated. His parents would be extremely cross that he had put himself in this situation by coming to talk to the boy. Weren't there stories of adults who used children as decoys to get people to open their gates so they could storm in? He should have stayed inside. Should he tell the boy to go next door where there would at least be an adult? But the boy had chosen to come here. Perhaps he had seen Rohan watching him from the car and knew this was his house.

'We stay there.' The boy pointed in the direction of the squatter camp. 'I go to school there.' He pointed in the direction of Mount View Primary. He was trying to reassure Rohan that it would be OK to open the gate. He was still in his school uniform but wore a pair of dirty-blue rubber sandals. His legs were as thin as sticks.

'Isn't there a doctor with your mother?' It was such a silly question that as soon as it was out, Rohan wished he could take it back. If they could afford a doctor, they wouldn't be squatters on a bare hillside. The boy shook his head vigorously. If he thought it was stupid, he didn't let it show on his troubled face.

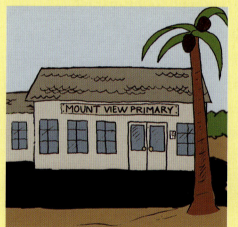

'Wait there!' Rohan returned to the house. The button for the electric gate was inside the front door. The boy waited while the wrought-iron bars slowly rolled back.

'OK. Bring your buckets over here.' Rohan pointed to the outside tap. The buckets clanked against each other as the boy jogged towards him.

'Thank you,' he said quietly.

The unexpected softness in his voice had a strange effect on Rohan. It sounded so different from his own bossy tone. Suddenly he felt a little ashamed. This was the same boy whose wire cars he admired! If he were still at Mount View Primary they would probably be in the same class. They might even have been friends and he would be learning how to make wire cars himself. Why had he spoken so arrogantly? It was really only a small favour that was being asked for. The water in the bucket gurgling and churning reminded Rohan of the water swirling beneath the Mozambican woman with her baby. *Her* rescuer had been taking a really big risk but hadn't looked big-headed. He had just got on with the job.

Under your skin

When both buckets were full, the boy stooped to lift one on to his head. Rohan saw his face and neck muscles strain under the weight. How would he manage to keep it balanced and carry the other bucket too?

'Wait! I'll give you a hand.' Rohan's offer was out before he had time to think it through properly. If the boy was surprised, he didn't show it. All his energy seemed to be focused on his task. Rohan dashed into the kitchen to grab the spare set of keys. Ma would be away for another hour at least. He would be back soon and she need never know. It was only after the gate clicked behind them, that Rohan remembered the neighbours. If anyone saw him, they were bound to ask Ma what he was doing with a boy from the squatter camp. He crossed the fingers of one hand.

At first Rohan said nothing. Sharing the weight of the bucket, he could feel the strain all the way up from his fingers to his left shoulder. When they reached the corner and set off down the hill, the bucket seemed to propel them forward. It was an effort to keep a steady pace. Rohan glanced at the container on the boy's head, marvelling at how he kept it balanced. He caught the boy's eye.

'How do you do that? You haven't spilt a drop!'

The boy gave a glimmer of a smile.

'You learn.'

Rohan liked the simple reply. He should ask the boy about the cars. This was his chance, before they turned into the noisy main road and reached the squatter camp.

'I've seen you with wire cars. Do you make them yourself?'

'Yes – and my brother.'

'You make them together? Do you keep them all?'

'My brother – he sells them at the beach.' The boy waved his free hand in the direction of the sea. 'The tourists – they like them.'

'Your cars are better than any I've seen in the shops! Do you get lots of money for them?'

'Mmhh!' The boy made a sound something between a laugh and a snort. Rohan realised that he had asked another brainless question. Would they be staying in a shack if they had lots of money? Rohan had often seen his own father bargaining to get something cheaper from a street hawker. He tried to cover his mistake.

'There's a shop in the Mall where they sell wire cars. They charge a lot and yours are a hundred times better!'

'We can't go there. The guards – they don't let us in.'

English Works

Rohan knew the security guards at the entrance to the Mall. Some of them even greeted his parents with a little salute. Rohan had seen poor children hanging around outside. They offered to push your trolley, to clean your car – anything for a few cents. Sometimes Ma gave an orange or an apple from her shopping bag to a child. Other times she would just say 'No thank you' and wave a child away. Ma never gave money. She said they might spend it on drugs. Rohan had never thought what it would be like to be chased away. How did the guards decide who could enter? How could the boy and his brother go and show the lady in the African Crafts shop his cars if they weren't allowed in?

Rohan was quiet as they reached the main road and turned towards the squatter camp. The noise of vehicles roaring past was deafening. He never normally walked down here. Not by himself nor with anyone else. His family went everywhere by car. With all the locks down, of course. The only people who walked were poor people. His eyes were drawn to a group of young men walking towards them. They were still some distance away but already Rohan began to feel uneasy. They were coming from the crossroads that his dad always approached on full alert. Rohan knew how his father jumped the red lights when the road was clear, especially at night. Everyone had heard stories of gangs who hijacked cars waiting for the lights to change.

The handle had begun to feel like it was cutting into his fingers. The boy must have sensed something because he signalled to Rohan to lower the bucket. For a few seconds they each stretched their fingers.

'It's too far? You want to go?' The boy was giving him a chance to change his mind. To leave and go back home. He had already helped carry the water more than half way. He could make an excuse about the time. But the thought of running back to the house along the road on his own now worried him.

'No, it's fine. Let's go.' Rohan heard a strange brightness in his own voice. He curled his fingers around the handle again.

As they drew nearer the men, Rohan felt their gaze on him and suddenly his head was spinning with questions. Why on earth had he offered to help carry the water? What did he think he was doing coming down here? And he hadn't even yet entered the squatter camp itself!

'We go here.' The boy's voice steadied him a little.

Under your skin

TASK

❶ Read the text carefully. Working in pairs and using a copy of the story, highlight and add comments about what you find out about Rohan and Solani. What do you learn about their lifestyles – their schooling, family lives, interests?

❷ Focus on two or three of the parts you have highlighted and discuss the impact of the words and phrases the author has used. How has the writer's South African culture influenced her language and style? Add further annotations to your copy of the story.

❸ Complete a copy of the chart below, comparing the different lives of the two boys:

	Similarities	Differences
Physical appearance		
Schooling		
Home and lifestyle		
Interests		
Opportunities		
Other aspects?		

❹ Next, still in your pair, identify ways in which Rohan's feelings change during the extract. Use the cards supplied by your teacher to help you to identify specific feelings at different points in the text. Highlight important quotations in the story. Report back to the rest of the class.

❺ Finally, write a formal essay:

In the short story *Out of Bounds*, how does Beverley Naidoo describe Rohan's experience of two cultures?

Remember to use quotations to support your ideas and to discuss the effect these have on the reader.

English Works

Focus on poetry

You will now study a range of poems from different cultural contexts. To begin with, you will explore the use of dialect and Standard English in a bit more detail. Next, you will discuss some extracts from poems, focusing on how the language and style of the poems affect the reader. After this introductory work, you will work together in groups, to explore the features of a particular poem and poet, which you will then present to the rest of the class.

Exploring dialect

As explained earlier, dialect is a distinctive version of a language with its own vocabulary and grammar. Different parts of the United Kingdom, for example, have their own words for things (e.g. barmcakes in Manchester, not rolls) or their own grammatical constructions (e.g. 'I didn't do nothing' in the South East). There are also variations between countries speaking the same language: for example, trainers are called 'sneakers' in America and 'takkies' in South Africa.

Both Standard English and dialect users may speak with a strong accent. When dialect is written down, unconventional spelling may be used to show how it is pronounced.

TASK

1. In pairs, read out loud the following examples of Afro-Caribbean, black British and Jamaican dialect out loud. Then re-write them in Standard English:

   To cut a laang story short I want to see de children wake up happy.

   I seh get rid of weapons, every one a dem. Mek we free de masses.

   Di grass turn brown an soh many trees cut down.

   Yu did yu time pan ert, yu nevah get yu just dizert.

   Mi know yu couldn tek it, di anguish an di pain.

   Mi struggling in vain fi mek enz meet.

   Mi revalueshanary fren pauz awhile den him look mi in mi eye.

   Mi av mi rezavaeshans bout de cansiquenses an implicaeshans espehshally fi black libahraeshan.

English Works

Under your skin

> ### TASK continued
>
> ❷ Working in pairs, discuss:
>   - ❏ What changes to vocabulary and grammar did you make when you 'translated' the dialect into Standard English?
>   - ❏ What was lost in the translation into Standard English?
>
>   Report your findings to the class.
>
> ❸ Now write your own definitions of dialect, Standard English and Creole. Include some examples to illustrate each of them.

You are now going to consider a range of extracts from poems from different cultures and traditions. All of the poets have used language in specific ways to make their point or convey their cultural identity. Remember that words often have several layers of meaning, so, as you read, consider the connotations or implications of words. What impact do these words have on the reader? Do they mean something specific in that writer's culture?

Several of the poets also choose to assert their cultural identity through using non-Standard English. Their dialect is a strong part of their background and heritage. Poets often use dialect to celebrate their culture, connect with their past, and 'give voice' to their ideas, particularly if these take the form of protest. Their use of dialect adds to the richness of the poetry; the reader is almost able to hear the poets giving expression to their ideas.

When considering the poems, look out for other techniques as well as dialect. For example, consider the punctuation and the length of lines.

TASK

❶ Read 'Somehow we survive' by Dennis Brutus on the following page.

❷ Look carefully at the annotations that have been made.

Dennis Brutus

English Works 137

Somehow we survive – Dennis Brutus

Patrols uncoil along the asphalt dark
hissing their menace to our lives,

most cruel, all our land is scarred with terror,
rendered unlovely and unlovable;
sundered are we and all our passionate surrender

but somehow tenderness survives.

*Snake metaphor with use of 'hissing' and 'uncoil' – suggests the fear with which the people of South Africa regarded the military or police during Apartheid.

*Choice of 'menace' reinforces the threat of the 'patrols'. 'Menace' has connotations of evil, unjustified interference.

*Interesting 'asphalt dark' rather than tarred roads. The sibilance (hissing sound) of the first syllable of 'asphalt' works well with the snake metaphor as this is continued in 'hissing' and 'menace'.

*Putting 'most cruel' at the start of the second stanza, separated by commas, gives it emphasis. 'Cruel' adds to the connotations of the snake metaphor used in the first stanza.

*'Terror' implies the heartlessness and cruelty of the state. It is ironic that the state, which is meant to protect, is the cause of the land being 'scarred with terror'. The use of 'scarred' conveys how deeply the 'menace' and violence has affected the lives of the country/the people.

*'Sundered' is a particularly violent verb, which means torn apart/severed.

*The extract is even more poignant because it is one sentence, which echoes how the aggression has infiltrated everyone's lives, but not necessarily their souls. By the time the reader has reached the end of this sentence we agree with the poet that it is indeed remarkable that 'somehow' – against the odds – 'tenderness survives'.

*The last line, as a separate stanza, is a complete contrast to what's come before. 'But' signals a different or unexpected view, reinforced by the gentleness of the choice of 'tenderness', which further emphasises all the evil, threat and violence in the rest of the poem.

*The use of 'unlovely' and 'unlovable' in the one line reinforces the idea that there is an absence of love here, that it is the state's fault that the country is in this condition.

English Works

Under your skin

TASK

Now read and discuss the following extracts from poems. You will be studying these in more detail later. Bearing in mind the annotations around 'Somehow we survive', focus particularly on the impact of each poet's choice of language.

'Blowing in a Random Breeze' – Amryl Johnson

Whitewash the face of hunger
When all the features have been removed
Paint on the smile, the laughing eyes
Show the tourists what they want
But not too close
Behind the grinning façade are slums
Which rob the people of all dignity.

'Time Come' – Linton Kwesi Johnson

now yu si fire burning in mi eye,
smell badness pan mi bret
feel vialence, vialence,
burstin outta mi;
look out!
it too late now:
I did warn yu.

'Caribbean Woman Prayer' – Grace Nichols

Wake up Lord
brush di sunflakes from yuh eye
back de sky a while Lord
an hear dis Mother-woman
on behalf of her pressure-down people

English Works 139

Get Up, Stand Up – Bob Marley

Get up, stand up: stand up for your rights!

Get up, stand up: don't give up the fight!

Get up, stand up: stand up for your rights!

Get up, stand up: don't give up the fight!

Most people think

Great God will come from the skies,

Take away everything

And make everybody feel high.

But if you know what life is worth,

You will look for yours on earth:

And now you see the light,

You stand up for your rights. Jah!

Under your skin

Your next task is to prepare a group presentation about one of the poems and the poet. Your presentation should focus on how the writer's background has influenced the language and style of the text. You need to bring out how the writer's choice of language makes a point about their culture.

TASK

1. Working in small groups, read the complete version of the poem supplied by your teacher.
2. Research the background of the poet and the social and political history of the country they come from. Note key points.
3. Re-read the poem several times. In your group, discuss and make notes on the key features of the poem. You may wish to focus on some of the following features:
   - Spelling variations
   - Unconventional punctuation, including use of lower-case letters and lack of full stops
   - Grammatical changes. Look out for omissions (words which are left out) and different forms of verbs, determiners (the, this) and pronouns (me, you)
   - The structure of the poem – regular and irregular stanzas, repetition, refrains
   - The sounds of the poem, including the poet's use of rhyme, alliteration, assonance, and onomatopoeia
   - The rhythm(s) of the language used. Consider the length of lines and words used, and how these affect the rhythm
   - Symbolism, including use of imagery (personification, metaphor and simile)
   - Imperative (commanding) verb forms and how these affect the tone
   - Hyphenated words which link two ideas together

   Remember, for each language feature you identify, you need to explore *what it conveys about the poet's culture* and *the effect on the reader*. Refer back to the annotated extract from 'Somehow we survive' to see examples of this.
4. Decide on how you are going to sequence all your different points about the poet and the poem. Start with information about the poet then deal with aspects of the poem. At the end, sum up key points about culture and language.
5. Working as a group, prepare and deliver your presentation.
6. As other groups deliver their presentations, note the key points made about language and style. How are the poets and poems different?

English Works

In the next part of this unit, you will be writing a Year 9 pupil's guide to the extract from the poem 'Letter from Mama Dot' by Fred D'Aguiar. This task will be a useful introduction to the sort of work you will do in your forthcoming GCSE course. You will need to draw on what you have already learned in this unit about culture, language and style.

From 'Letter from Mama Dot' – Fred D'Aguiar

Born on a sunday
in the kingdom of Ashante

Sold on a monday
into slavery

Ran away on tuesday
cause she born free

Lost a foot on wednesday
when they catch she

Worked all thursday
till her head grey

Dropped on friday
where they buried she

Freed on saturday
into a new century

English Works

Under your skin

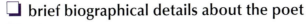

TASK

1. **Research** the background to the poet and the poem. Your research should include:
   - ❑ brief biographical details about the poet
   - ❑ an overview of the historical and social context that influenced the poet's writing
2. **Plan** your work carefully before you start writing. Decide how you are going to structure your guide and think about how you will link your ideas so they are clear to your reader.

Your guide needs to include a **detailed analysis of the poem**, explaining:

- The poet's **message**
- The **structure** of the poem
- The poet's **use of language**
- The **ways in which the poet's culture, traditions and context have influenced the language and style of the poem**

TASK

3. Now **write** your guide. Remember to **check** your work carefully once you have completed the task. Ensure that your spelling, punctuation and grammar are as accurate as possible. This will help you convey your points about the poem in a convincing way.

English Works

The power of speech

In the final section of this unit you will focus on extracts from four powerful speeches, made by political leaders in America, Africa and Burma, which span more than a century.

1. Read the first speech by Chief Joseph.
2. What is his message? What does he say about his culture, traditions, heritage?

3. Which words and phrases do you find particularly powerful? Why? How does he try to persuade his audience?

Chief Joseph (1879)

In this extract Chief Joseph, chief of one of the native American tribes, was talking to the American president, asking that his people be allowed to return to their homelands:

> *Treat all men alike. Give them the same law. Give them all an even chance to live and grow. All men were made by the same Great Spirit Chief. They are all brothers.*
>
> *You might as well expect the rivers to run backward as that any man who was born free should be contented penned up and denied liberty to go where he pleases. Let me be a free man – free to travel, free to stop, free to work, free to trade where I choose; free to choose my own teachers, free to follow the religion of my fathers, free to think and talk and act for myself – and I will obey every law, or submit to the penalty.*

Now read the following speeches:

Martin Luther King (1963)

Here, Doctor Martin Luther King, who was awarded the Nobel Peace Prize the following year, is talking at a Civil Rights demonstration in Washington:

> I say to you today, my friends, so even though we face the difficulties of today and tomorrow, I still have a dream. It is a dream rooted in the American dream.
>
> I have a dream that one day this nation will rise up and live out the true meaning of its creed: 'We hold these truths to be self-evident; that all men are treated equal.'

English Works

> I have a dream that one day on the red hills of Georgia the sons of former slaves and the sons of former slave owners will be able to sit down together at the table of brotherhood.
>
> I have a dream that one day even the state of Mississippi, a state sweltering with the heat of injustice, sweltering with the heat of oppression, will be transformed into an oasis of freedom and justice.
>
> I have a dream that my four little children will one day live in a nation where they will not be judged by the colour of their skin but by the content of their character.
>
> I have a dream today.

Nelson Mandela (1964)

In this extract Nelson Mandela, leader of the African National Congress, who was on trial for treason against the apartheid government of South Africa, tells the court about the hopes and aspirations of the African people. In spite of being imprisoned for more than 30 years, Nelson Mandela was awarded the Nobel Peace Prize for his role in working with the South African government to end apartheid in 1994:

> Africans want a just share in the whole of South Africa; they want security and a stake in society. Above all, we want equal political rights, because without them our disabilities will be permanent. I know this sounds revolutionary to the whites in this country, because the majority of voters will be Africans. This makes the white man fear democracy…
>
> This then is what the ANC is fighting for. Their struggle is a truly national one. It is a struggle of the African people, inspired by their own suffering and their own experience. It is a struggle for the right to live.
>
> During my lifetime I have dedicated myself to this struggle of the African people. I have fought against white domination, and I have fought against black domination. I have cherished the ideal of a democratic and free society in which all persons live together in harmony and with equal opportunities. It is an ideal which I hope to live for and to achieve. But if needs be, it is an ideal for which I am prepared to die.

Aung San Suu Kyi (1995)

Aung San Suu Kyi, the leader of the pro-democracy opposition party in Burma, was under house arrest for several years. She speaks here in a video address when she was awarded the Nobel Peace Prize:

> The last six years have afforded me much time and food for thought. I came to the conclusion that the human race is not divided into two opposing camps of good and evil. It is made up of those who are capable of learning and those who are incapable of doing so. Here I am not talking of learning in the narrow sense of acquiring an academic education, but of learning as the process of absorbing those lessons of life that enable us to increase peace and happiness in our world. Women in their roles as mothers have traditionally assumed the responsibility of teaching children values that will guide them throughout their lives. It is time we were given the full opportunity to use our natural teaching skills to contribute towards building a modern world that can withstand the tremendous challenges of the technological revolution which in turn has brought revolutionary change in social values...
>
> These, then, are our common hopes that unite us — that as the shackles of prejudice and intolerance fall from our own limbs we can strive to identify and remove the impediments to human development everywhere. The mechanisms by which this great task is to be achieved provided the proper focus of this great Forum. I feel sure that women throughout the world who, like me, cannot be with you, join me in sending you all our prayers and good wishes for a joyful and productive meeting.
>
> I thank you.

Under your skin

❶ In groups, discuss the speeches. What are the key ideas in each one? Have the speakers' concerns changed between 1879 (Chief Joseph) and 1995 (Aung San Suu Kyi)? To what extent are the different speeches explicitly about or influenced by culture and tradition?

❷ Discuss the techniques that are used to persuade the audience. Are there words or phrases that have a particular impact? Do they have particular connotations or implications?

Note key points in a copy of the grid below:

	Chief Joseph	Martin Luther King	Nelson Mandela	Aung San Suu Kyi
Emotive vocabulary				
Imagery				
Pattern of three etc.				

❸ In your group, consider your completed grid and discuss whether there are any common features of language and style.

Next, you will prepare a presentation of one of the speeches for the rest of the class. You will need to think carefully about the impact of specific words and phrases, and how you will convey the ideas of the speech most effectively.

TASK

❶ Select one of the speeches to deliver and carefully annotate a copy of it. You need to indicate:
- ❏ where you will emphasise words
- ❏ where it may be appropriate to use gestures
- ❏ where it will be particularly effective to look at your audience
- ❏ where you need to pause
- ❏ parts that need to be read slowly and parts that could be read more quickly or at a steady pace

❷ Working in a small group, practise delivering part of your speech, applying the ideas you have noted.

English Works

TASK continued

3. Deliver your speech to the group. Evaluate each other's work, then work further on improving the delivery of your speech.
4. Select the most effective presenter in the group to deliver their speech to the class.
5. Listen to the selected speeches. Evaluate how successfully they were delivered, referring to the points below. Were there other features used by presenters that were also effective?

Look for evidence of the following:

- eye contact
- gesture
- body language
- volume
- intonation
- pace/timing
- expression
- dramatic pauses
- voice inflection
- emphasis
- rhythm/cadence (rise and fall in pitch of voice)

TASK

Your final task in this unit is to write a comparison of at least two of the four speeches you looked at earlier in the unit. You could organise your essay like this:

1. Introduction – explain the purpose of your piece of writing
2. Analysis of first speech – comment on its main features and impact
3. Analysis of second speech – comment on features and bring out how it is similar/different
4. Concluding comments – comment on which speech has more impact and why

Make sure you discuss similarities and differences between the speeches. Focus on:
- ❏ the purpose of each one
- ❏ the vocabulary used and its impact on the reader/audience
- ❏ ways in which the writer/speaker has tried to persuade the reader/audience
- ❏ ways in which the language and style have been influenced by cultural context
- ❏ the overall impact of each speech

English Works

UNIT 8 Self review

Your work will be assessed in a number of ways throughout key stage 3. For example:

✓ Your teacher might talk to you about your work and suggest ways in which you might improve it

✓ You might be asked to work with a partner to make constructive comments about each other's drafted work

✓ You might be asked as a class to comment on a group presentation given by members of your class

✓ You might be set a test which will be marked by your teacher

✓ You might be asked to record some of your recent spelling errors and then think of strategies to learn those words which you find difficult

✓ Your teacher might write a comment at the end of a piece of work that you have done

It is very important, however, that you are fully involved in your own learning. You need to think about your strengths as a reader, writer and speaker and listener. You also need to think about areas which you need to improve. You need to be involved in the process of setting targets which will help you and your teacher to enable you to make progress in certain areas. This short unit focuses on this process.

English Works

Myself as a reader	Level 4	Level 5	Level 6
What type of texts do I read?	I can read a range of texts with support	I can read a range of texts in class and at home	I read a wide range of texts independently
How well do I understand what I read?	I understand the main ideas, themes, events and characters I am beginning to read between the lines	I understand the main features, themes and characters I can use inference and deduction to read between the lines	I can identify layers of meaning and understand why they are important
How well can I find information from texts?	I can find and use ideas and information	I can retrieve and gather information from a range of sources	I can summarise a range of information from different sources

English Works

Self review

What sort of reference do I make to the text?	I can refer to the text to explain my views	I can refer to words, phrases and sentences in the text to support my views	I can refer to the language, themes and structure of a text to justify my views
What do I understand about the choices made by writers?	I tend to describe what has happened in a text	I am aware of some of the ways the text might affect the reader	I am aware that the writer has chosen words and sentences to create a particular effect for the reader

Review your work as a reader. Which statements best describe you? You may find that your achievement is uneven and your skills might not fit neatly into one level descriptor.

Identify your strengths as well as areas you need to improve.

Now set yourself three targets which will help you to either:

● achieve a level which is not yet quite secure, or
● achieve a higher level by the end of Year 9.

English Works

Myself as a writer	Level 4	Level 5	Level 6
How do I organise my ideas?	I organise my ideas appropriately for my readers

I can sustain and develop my ideas | I generally organise my ideas into paragraphs when appropriate | I organise and structure my ideas clearly into paragraphs |
| What kinds of words do I use? | I can be quite adventurous in my choice of words

I try to choose words which will create a particular effect | My choice of vocabulary is imaginative

I use words precisely | I can use a varied vocabulary to create particular effects

I can use an impersonal style when appropriate |
| What kinds of sentences do I use? | I am beginning to use complex sentences in order to extend my ideas | I use both simple and complex sentences | I use a range of sentence structures, including simple, compound and complex |
| How do I punctuate my writing? | I can use full stops, capital letters and question marks correctly

I am beginning to use punctuation inside sentences | I can use a range of punctuation including commas, apostrophes and inverted commas. I usually use these correctly | I can use a range of punctuation to make my meaning clear. I usually use these correctly |
| How good is my spelling? | I can usually spell simple words as well as words with a large number of syllables | I can usually spell words which have more complex regular patterns | My spelling is generally accurate

I can spell words which are irregular |

English Works

Self review

What is my handwriting like?	My handwriting is joined, fluent and legible	My handwriting is joined, clear and fluent	My handwriting is neat, fluent and legible
		I can adapt it to a range of tasks	
How aware am I of my readers?	My writing is lively and thoughtful	My writing is varied and interesting	My writing engages and sustains the reader's interest
	I try to develop my ideas in ways that are interesting for the reader	I can write in a range of forms for different readers	I can adapt the way I write depending on my audience and purpose
		I can write in a more formal style when appropriate	I can use a more impersonal style when appropriate

Review your work as a writer. Which statements best describe you? You may find that your achievement is uneven and your skills might not fit neatly into one level descriptor.

Identify your strengths as well as areas you need to improve.

Now set yourself three targets which will help you to either:

- achieve a level which is not yet quite secure, or
- achieve a higher level by the end of Year 9.

English Works

Myself as a speaker and listener	Level 4	Level 5	Level 6
What sort of situations am I confident in?	I can talk and listen with confidence in an increasing range of situations	I can talk and listen confidently in a wide range of situations I am confident when speaking in more formal situations	I can adapt my talk to different situations with confidence
How aware am I of my listeners?	I can adapt my talk to my audience and purpose	I can engage the interest of my listeners	I can engage the interest of my listeners
How well do I collaborate in groups?	I listen carefully to others and can respond to their views I can ask questions and make contributions	I pay close attention to what others say and take account of their views I can ask questions and make contributions that help to develop the discussion	I take an active part in discussions I am sensitive towards others in the group and show that I understand their ideas

English Works

Self review

How well do I express myself?	I can describe events and give clear opinions	I am beginning to vary my vocabulary and expression	I am able to use a good variety of vocabulary and expression
	I can develop my ideas thoughtfully		
Am I able to use Standard English when appropriate?	I can use some of the features of Standard English	I am beginning to use Standard English in formal situations	I use Standard English in formal situations

Review your work as a speaker and listener. Which statements best describe you? You may find that your achievement is uneven and your skills might not fit neatly into one level descriptor.

Identify your strengths as well as areas you need to improve.

Now set yourself three targets which will help you to either:

- achieve a level which is not yet quite secure, or
- achieve a higher level by the end of Year 9.

English Works

SMART targets

Specific
A vague target such as 'I want to improve my writing' won't help you. Make your targets specific, for example, 'I will use a range of simple and complex sentences in my writing.'

Measurable
How will you know whether you have achieved your target? A specific target such as 'I will use the LOOK, SAY, COVER, WRITE, CHECK method to learn six spellings every week' will be easy to measure. Your teacher will also be able to help you.

Achievable
Make sure that you don't set yourself targets that are way beyond your reach at the moment. Take things a step at a time. If you're a Level 4 writer and you want to be Level 6 next month, that's probably a little unrealistic; you'll just end up feeling demotivated. Set your sights just a little higher than where you are at the moment.

Relevant
Make sure that the target you set yourself is really appropriate for you. Don't aim to improve your spelling if it's really paragraphs that you are struggling with!

Time-bonded
We're all very good at putting things off and there are some jobs that just never seem to get done! Make sure that you set yourself a reasonable time limit, for example, 'By the end of term I will be organising my ideas into paragraphs in 9/10 pieces of written work.'

Remember – be SMART!